SOLDIER

From Script To Screen

by

Danny Stewart

Front Cover Design by Daniel Swanson - website: https://van-garde.com/

The image on Front Cover Silhouette of a soldier against the sunrise. ©iStockphoto/vadimrysev

Art by ©Getty Images/iStockphoto

First Edition, 2023

BearManor Media

ISBN: 979-8-88771-113-3

Dedicated to David Webb Peoples and my grandfather,
Thomas O'Callaghan.
His favourite motion picture was Unforgiven.

The Grandparents of Danny Stewart

TABLE OF CONTENTS

ACKNOWLEDGMENTS

First and foremost, I'd like to thank screenwriter David Webb Peoples for his time, generosity, and for providing me with his original script for *Soldier*. I had many conversations on the phone with David. His conceit for the picture fascinates me. Like so many films he has penned in his career, from *Blade Runner*, *Unforgiven*, and *Twelve Monkeys*, *Soldier* remains provocative and highly resonant.

I'd like to give a special mention to production designer David L. Snyder. In 1980, Snyder worked with Ridley Scott on *Blade Runner*, for which he received an Academy Award nomination with production designer Lawrence G. Paull. Snyder's stunning work for *Soldier* is a key component in the piece. Snyder has been of vital importance to this book and has given much support and time. He literally gave me everything he had. I have VHS tapes from behind the scenes that have never seen the light of day, as well as photos, production art, and his original cinema ticket from the premiere.

I'd like to thank other key participants from the cast and crew who were instrumental in the construction of *Soldier's Journey*: Fred Fontana, Allen Easton, Dennis Maguire, Andy Spilkoman, Jayson Merrill, Phil Shanahan, Eric Dyson, Mark Bringleson, Mike Fantasia, Kim Bailey, Jon Danniells, Peter Montagna, Steve LaPorte, Van Ling, Ron Phillips , Warner Bros., Morgan Creek, and Paul M. Sammon, author of *Future Noir: The Making of Blade Runner*, for his continuing guidance and support. I have never been alone in my fascination with this motion picture. I'd also like to thank John Hansen, Mark Stratton, and John Kenneth Muir—three writers who have published excellent and insightful material and allowed me to utilize it within the pages of this book.

AUTHOR INTRODUCTION

by Danny Stewart

I wanted to craft this book to write about and archive the evolution of the Western genre and uncover the making of *Soldier*. I am infatuated with the concept that screenwriter David Webb Peoples envisioned for the project. I've had the opportunity to read his original screenplay, and it's not hyperbole to declare it a true genre *landmark*. I wanted to broaden and better educate readers about the process and the sheer scale and amount of work it took to create this particular motion picture.

I think it is a high-quality film that is overlooked. There are many virtues from David L. Snyder's production design extrapolated with an industrialist aesthetic, one in which a junkyard planet looms over the action. It is drearily perfect and it recapitulates the life of homesteaders in the West with the colonists and, at the same time, with the equally dehumanizing vision of a future run purely on militarism and war. British cinematographer David Tattersall's spot-on lighting reinforces both the sense of inhumanity and gradual humanization of the world and character of *Soldier*. The music by Joel McNeely itself does a fine job reflecting the main character and story of the movie.

The film is a part military movie, part Western, and part outsider allegory, in many respects. As the story progresses, McNeely's score becomes more militaristic and rousing, yet more gentle and hopeful. McNeely uses rhythmic brass and percussion reminiscent of Jerry Goldsmith while riffing on the music of the *Alien* and *Predator* movies.

Kurt Russell's role as Todd—what a challenge it was for an actor to have to have only 104 words of dialogue and pull the whole thing off with the physicality of his performance. I think that is an amazing feat. What Russell does is a difficult job, even though people might think that he conveys so much with a character who has been raised from birth to be machine-like. The acting icon anchors the film through his tears, emotion, facial expressions, movement, and gestures.

Directed by Paul W.S. Anderson, whose credits include *Shopping*, the hit videogame adaptation *Mortal Kombat* (1995), and *Event Horizon* (1997). Each of those projects display Paul's great visual sense, and all were extremely well-shot pictures. The initial critical consensus, and box office receipts for *Solider* suggested the movie itself belonged in the junkyard, much like its character. It's a shame the film was a flop, lost like tears in the rain. It deserves to be reappraised, re-evaluated, and rediscovered. Such a reappraisal has been gearing up in recent years regarding the film's subtext, spirituality, and soul. I'm excited to have crafted this book on the subject with brand new cast and crew interviews.

The Western and Science Fiction Genre The Birth of A Sub-Genre

The hallmarks of the Western contain horses, guns, frontier towns, gunfights, cowboys, lawlessness, and, of course, plenty of whiskey. The Western genre was once a popular and financially-successful film genre in Hollywood for a number of decades. In the 1950s, Hollywood produced more Western movies than all other genres combined with the John Wayne pictures *Red River* (1948), *Rio Grande* (1950), *The Searchers* (1956), and *Rio Bravo* (1959). In the 1960s and 1970s, Wayne starred in many more Westerns, including such iconic pictures as *The Comancheros* (1961), *The Man Who Shot Liberty Valance* (1962), and *True Grit* (1969). Clint Eastwood, Randolph Scott, and directors like Howard Hawks, Sergio Leone, and Sam Peckinpah—all associated primarily with the Western genre—became household names.

Also, Japanese director Akira Kurosawa's influence on Western films and Western directors cannot be understated. His epic masterpieces, such as *Rashomon (1950), Seven Samurai (1954),* and *Yojimbo (1960)*, have been remade into Westerns. *The Outrage (1964)* is an American remake of Kurosawa's *Rashomon; The Magnificent Seven* (1960) is a remake of Kurosawa's *Seven Samurai,* replacing the samurai with cowboys; Sergio Leone's Spaghetti Western, *A Fistful of Dollars* (1967) is a remake of *Yojimbo.*

The Eastwood character, who became to be called The Man with No Name, shares the same traits as the lead character in *Yojimbo. But* instead of wielding a katana, Eastwood's character uses a revolver. Decades after *A Fistful of Dollars,* Walter Hill's *Last Man Standing (1996),* starring Bruce Willis in a Prohibition-era America, was released. Hill's film is another retelling of *Yojimbo*. Albert Pyun's futuristic cult sci-fi film *Omega Doom* (1996), a Rutger Hauer-starrer about a robot warrior playing both sides of a robot civil war, is also pure *Yojimbo.*

The Western genre drastically slowed down in the 1970s and 1980s, which led to the birth and evolution of a new sub-genre, the Space Opera. George Lucas's *Star Wars: Episode IV: A New Hope (1977)* is credited with starting this massively popular genre. George Lucas, the writer/director of *Star Wars*, has acknowledged having borrowed the idea from Kurosawa's samurai classic, *The Hidden Fortress* (1958). Also, Harrison Ford's character, Han Solo, is very much the epitome of a gunslinger cowboy. With this entry, sci-fi replaced the Western as an essential genre.

Then filmmaker George Miller created his first *Mad Max* (1979) picture, which, in many ways, is the equivalent to Leone's *Dollars* films, transposing the Western on wheels. He would then follow with *Mad Max 2: The Road Warrior* (1981), which in many ways echoes *For A Few Dollars More.* Also, the relationship between Max and the feral kid evokes George Stevens' Western, *Shane* (1953), and the climactic tanker chase was heavily influenced by John Ford's Western, *Stagecoach* (1939), in which the Apache's pursue the stagecoach.

Mad Max Beyond Thunderdome (1985), the third entry in the series, is representative of *The Good, The Bad, and The Ugly* (1966). It harkens back to that picture's moral dichotomy, in this case with the characters of "Mad" Max Rockatansky being The Good, Aunty Entity as The Bad, and Master Blaster as The Ugly. Instead of being set against the backdrop of the Civil War, Miller's film is set in a post-apocalyptic Australia. When introducing Max to the Thunderdome crowd in the film, Dr. Dealgood calls him The Man with No Name, which is a clear reference to Eastwood's character in the Leone "spaghetti Westerns." At the time of *Mad Max: Fury Road* (2015)'s release, director Miller described the film's key theme as being survival, which he believed to be the reason [1]"why the American Western was such a staple for the better part of a century in American cinema." The forthcoming Mad Max Furiosa (2023) will no doubt be the equivalent of Leone's *A Fistful of Dynamite* (1971).

Outland (1981) is a space Western that bears thematic resemblances to *High Noon* (1952). Rather than being set in a town on the American frontier, *Outland* takes place on the remote moon of Io, circling Jupiter, where Marshal William O'Neil, played by Sean Connery, has been assigned as the chief police officer on the mining colony. *Outland's* director, Peter Hyams, originally conceived the film being set in the old West. "I wanted to do a Western," he explained in an [2]*Empire* interview. "Everybody said, 'You can't

---

[1] *Silas Lesnick "George Miller Interview: Hope and Fear on Fury Road" (13 May, 2015)*

[2] *"Peter Hyams Film by Film" Empire accessed (30 July, 2014)*

do a Western; Westerns are dead; nobody will do a Western.' I remember thinking it was weird that this genre that had endured for so long was just gone. But then I woke up and concluded—obviously after other people—that it was alive and well, but in outer space. I wanted to make a film about the frontier. Not the wonder of it or its glamour: I wanted to do something about Dodge City and how hard life was."

Horror director John Carpenter used a similar approach he got into this business wanting to make Westerns, but they stopped making them—so he figured he had to find something he could do in this profession that was more popular than Westerns. And you might not think so, but there are a lot of similarities between Westerns and horror movies. They're both about archetypal characters, good and evil. So, he adapted. Nearly all of Carpenter's films are a compendium of Western underpinnings such as sieges, gunfights, a distrust of authority, and are throwbacks to the old-fashioned Westerns of Howard Hawks and John Ford. In 1976, Carpenter wrote, directed, scored, and edited *Assault on Precinct 13*. Carpenter's script, originally titled *The Anderson Alamo*, was heavily inspired by the Hawks Western *Rio Bravo*. He later directed a futuristic remake of the film with *Ghosts of Mars* (2001).

A number of Carpenter's biggest films—*Escape from New York* (1981), *The Thing* (1982), *Big Trouble in Little China* (1986), *They Live* (1988), *Escape From L.A* (1996) and *Vampires* (1998)—toy with Western conventions. On *Escape From New York's* inspiration, [3]Carpenter said, "I wrote *Escape From New York* way back in 1974; I believe I was inspired by the movie *Death Wish* (1974), which was very popular. I disagreed with its philosophy, taking the law into one's own hands, but the film came across with the sense of New York as a kind of jungle, and I wanted to make a SF film along those lines." By this time in the 80s, the genre had transformed into the urban Western.

Clint Eastwood's *Dirty Harry* films (1971-1988), Charles Bronson's *Death Wish* films (1974-1994), and Richard Donner's *Lethal Weapon* (1987) are contemporary Westerns. [4]Screenwriter Shane Black stated that his intention with *Lethal Weapon* was to do an "urban Western" inspired by *Dirty Harry* where a violent character "reviled for what he did, what he is capable of, the things he believed in" is eventually recruited for being the one who could solve the problem. The protagonists would be every-men policemen, "guys shuffling in a town like Los Angeles searching for something noble as justice when they're just guys in washed and worn suits seeking a paycheck." The

[3] *Samuel J. Maronie (April, 1981). "On the Set with Escape from New York". Starlog. No. 45.*

[4] *"Psycho Pension: The Genesis of Lethal Weapon". Lethal Weapon Collection (Documentary). Warner Bros. Home Entertainment. (2012)*

urban Western had evolved in Paul Verhoeven's *Robocop* (1987). The film is set in a futuristic Detroit of urban decay that very much reflects the past and present. There are many tropes of the Western genre at play as well. Robocop is a gunslinger, and Lewis is his faithful partner. The showdown between the resurrected Murphy and his killers evokes the Western classic *High Noon.*

With his film, *Cyborg* (1989), director Albert Pyun had envisioned the film as a futuristic Western. The film's Western influences include *The Searchers, Once Upon a Time in the West* (1968), and *Mad Max.* Van Damme's character is named Gibson, which is a nod to the Mad Max films (starring Mel Gibson). Heading into the 1990s, films like the revisionist Westerns (meaning the subversion of the standard format or theme of the Western) *Unforgiven* (1992) and *Tombstone* (1993) impacted the box office and held up extraordinarily. In 2004, *Unforgiven* was selected for preservation in the United States National Film Registry by the Library of Congress as being deemed "culturally, historically, or aesthetically significant."

With *The Quick and The Dead* (1995), director Sam Raimi and writer Simon Moore sought to pay homage to the Spaghetti Westerns of Leone. Instead of The traditional Western that generally focused on a strong, male lead, *The Quick and the Dead* subverted the genre by making the lead a female with Sharon Stone as "The Lady." Stone's character is a gunslinger who rides into the frontier town of Redemption, controlled by John Herod (played by Gene Hackman who also starred in *Unforgiven*). At the time, the film was not a success financially or critically. However, it has experienced a critical reassessment in the years following its release.

More recently, modern movie remakes, such as *3:10 To Yuma* (2007) and the Coen Brothers' *True Grit* (2010), have paid homage to their mid-20th century predecessors. These include *Cowboys & Aliens* (2011), *The Lone Ranger* (2013), and *Logan* (2017), which took thematic inspiration from the classic Western, *Shane.* The Western and Science Fiction genres will forever remain a staple in all aspects of storytelling and will continue to inspire countless new generations of filmmakers and screenwriters.

The Birth of An Actor – Kurt Russell An Overview of Career

Kurt Vogel Russell was born on March 17, 1951, in Springfield, Massachusetts. His father, Bing Russell, was an actor known for his work on *Bonanza* and *The Magnificent Seven* (1960). The elder Russell also guest-starred on many television shows, including *Playhouse 90, Highway Patrol, Wagon Train, The Life and Legend of Wyatt Earp, The Loretta Young Show, Johnny Ringo, Walt Disney's Wonderful World of Color, The Rifleman, Maverick, Zane Grey Theater, Route 66, Rawhide, Ben Casey, The Untouchables, Hazel, The Andy Griffith Show, The Twilight Zone, The Donna Reed Show, The Munsters, Gunsmoke, Combat!, Branded, The Fugitive, The Monkees, I Dream of Jeannie, Ironside, The Big Valley, Death Valley Days, Adam-12, The Virginian, Alias Smith and Jones, The Mod Squad, Mannix, The Rockford Files, The Streets of San Francisco, Emergency!,* and *Little House on the Prairie.*

Kurt's mum was a respected dancer named Louise Julia Russell. Kurt also had three sisters, Jilly, Jamie, and Jody.

The Russell family relocated to California when Kurt was a child. He and his siblings were raised in Los Angeles. Throughout his grade school years, he played little league baseball and later on high school baseball. Kurt went on to produce a documentary in 2014 called *The Battered Bastards of Baseball* about the Mavericks, a minor league baseball team in Portland, Oregon, that was owned by his father, Bing Russell. The documentary was positively received, and had a standing ovation at the 2014 Sundance Film Festival. It was clearly a tribute to the team and his family's legacy. Kurt had a baseball career in the 1970s, but tore a shoulder muscle and was forced to retire from the sport at the age of 22.

Although he appeared in an uncredited part, *It Happened at the World's Fair* (1963), marked Kurt's film debut. In the film, he played a boy who kicked Elvis Presley in the leg, which is particularly interesting because he would play Elvis later in his life. He would guest star in the ABC series *Our Man Higgins* a year later. He then played the title role in the series *The Travels of Jaimie McPheeters* (1963–64), which was based on Robert Lewis Taylor's Pulitzer Prize-winning novel.

Kurt guest-starred in the ABC series *The Fugitive* (1964) on the episode "Nemesis." He also played the mistaken orphan In NBC's series *The Virginian* in a pair of episodes ("A Father for Toby," 1964, and "The Brothers," 1965). At age 13, Kurt played the role of Jungle Boy on an episode of CBS's *Gilligan's Island* (1965). He played a similar role on the Western series *Gunsmoke* (1964) in the episode titled "Blue Heaven."

He then embarked upon a series of features for Disney. His Disney film debut was *Follow Me, Boys!* (1966). His other films for the company include *The Horse in the Gray Flannel Suit* (1969), *Guns in the Heather* (1969), *The Computer Wore Tennis Shoes* (1969), *The Barefoot Executive* (1971), *Now You See Him, Now You Don't* (1971), *Charley and the Angel* (1973), and *Superdad* (1973). He also narrated the animated short *Dad, Can I Borrow the Car?*, and voiced Copper in *The Fox and the Hound* (1980).

In addition to his film work, the actor also appeared in the Disney television shows *Willie and the Yank* and *The Secret of Boyne Castle.* Additionally, along with the Osmonds, Kurt cohosted the episode "Disneyland Showtime" on *The Wonderful World of Disney* (1970). He later returned to The Walt Disney Studios to star in Touchstone's *Captain Ron* (1992) and to play the world's most famous superhero in the Disney family comedy, *Sky High* (2005). Kurt appeared as Private Willie Prentiss in the episode "Willie and the Yank: The Mosby Raiders" on *Walt Disney's Wonderful World of Color.* (The episode was released theatrically in certain places as *Mosby's Marauders* (1967).

After that, Kurt continued to guest star on a number of television series. He, Jay C. Flippen, and Tom Tryon appeared in the "Charade of Justice" episode of the NBC series *The Road West.* On CBS's *Lost in Space* (episode "The Challenge"), Kurt appeared as Quano, the son of a planetary ruler. He met his future partner, Goldie Hawn, filming the Sherman Brothers' musical, *The One and Only, Genuine, Original Family Band* (1968). The pair also worked together in *Swing Shift* (1984), which Hawn both produced and starred in.

Kurt is best known for his collaborations with cult director John Carpenter playing such anti-hero roles as Snake Plissken (*Escape from New York*, 1981, and *Escape from LA*, 1996), RJ MacReady (*The Thing*, 1982), and truck driver Jack Burton (*Big Trouble in Little China*, 1986). He also appeared as the titular character in Carpenter's *Elvis* (1979), for which he received an Emmy nomination.

For his iconic turns as Snake Plissken, Kurt drew inspiration from Bruce Lee, Darth Vader, Clint Eastwood, and *The Exterminator* (1980). Speaking about his collaborations with Carpenter, Kurt has said, [5]"John's like that older brother that you know is smarter than you, but he lets you do the things you do well without making you feel he knows how to do them better. I like the way John's brain works. He has a unique, askew way of looking at a story."

[6]"Some of the crazy reviews we got on *Escape from LA*... 'Do Carpenter and Russell realize they've made a lefty movie?' That was my favorite of all," Kurt recalls. "Boy, did they not get it. That guy really didn't get it. His agenda is so in his face he can't get it's just about a guy who wants to have a cigarette! At the end of the movie, he just wants you to get out of his face! He blows the match out on you. Go home! Get away! Die! Leave me alone!" John Carpenter has frequently praised and admired the actor for his professionalism, and the fact that he isn't afraid to take on roles that will potentially damage his image or make him look foolish. In returning to the position of Snake Plissken in the sequel *Escape From LA*, Kurt found that his costume from the original film still fit 15 years later. He also co-wrote the script and conceived the ending. Although the film was received less favorably than the original, it has become recognized as a cult film and has received its due reappraisal over time. The role of Snake is a personal favorite of Kurt's. There have long been talks of either a forthcoming sequel (*Escape From Earth*), a remake, or a prequel. One can hope Kurt Russell returns to the classic anti-hero role he invented alongside legendary helmer John Carpenter.

Kurt played Olympic hockey coach Herb Brooks in the biographical drama *Miracle* (2004). The film tells the story of the "miracle on ice"—the gold-medal triumph of the American hockey team at the 1980 Winter Olympics. Another notable credit is *Silkwood* (1983), the biographical drama directed by Mike Nichols. Kurt starred alongside Meryl Streep and Cher, and received a Golden Globe nomination for Best Supporting Actor. In *Tequila Sunrise* (1988), written and directed by Robert Towne, Kurt starred alongside Mel Gibson and Michelle Pfeiffer, with Raul Julia, J. T. Walsh, Arliss Howard, and Gabriel Damon in supporting roles. Kurt modeled his character in the film, Detective Lieutenant Nick Frescia, after basketball coach Pat Riley, with his slicked-back hair. In a review for [7]*The Globe and Mail*

---

[5] *The Los Angeles Times (February 4, 1996)*

[6] *Personal quote from Kurt Russell source https://www.imdb.com/name/nm0000621/bio?ref_=nm_dyk_qu#quotes*

[7] *Jay Scott The Globe and Mail Toronto (December 2, 1988)*

(Toronto), critic Jay Scott wrote "Kurt Russell has never seemed more clever, Mel Gibson more vulnerable, nor Michelle Pfeiffer more goddess-like."

In the buddy cop film *Tango and Cash* (1989), Kurt starred with Sylvester Stallone, Jack Palance, and Teri Hatcher. Stallone and Russell play well off one another. Ron Howard's *Backdraft* (1991) tells the story of Chicago firefighters on the trail of a serial arsonist. The film starred William Baldwin, Scott Glenn, Jennifer Jason Leigh, Rebecca De Mornay, Donald Sutherland, Robert De Niro, Jason Gedrick, and J. T. Walsh.

The psychological thriller *Unlawful Entry* (1992) was directed by Jonathan Kaplan, and starred Madeleine Stowe and Ray Liotta. [8] *Variety's* Todd McCarthy wrote that despite being another film following in the mold of Fatal Attraction, it was "a very effective victimization thriller." McCarthy also praised Liotta and Russell's performances, as well as Kaplan's direction of the script into "areas of social and class-structure observations" when dealing with unhinged police figures in an urban setting.

Kurt gained rave reviews for his portrayal of Wyatt Earp in *Tombstone* (1993), a film which has become a cult classic. (I highly recommend checking out the book *The Making of Tombstone: Behind the Scenes of the Classic Modern Western* by John Farkis to learn more about the film.) Kurt also played Colonel "Jack" O'Neil in Roland Emmerich's second American film, the Science fiction adventure *Stargate* (1994). Then he played Dr. David Grant, a consultant for U.S. Army Intelligence in the action film *Executive Decision* (1996). In Jonathan Mostow's tour-de-force thriller *Breakdown* (1997), Kurt worked alongside J.T. Walsh again. The film is another classic and one of this author's favorite Kurt Russell performances.

In *Soldier* (1998), he played a bred-born soldier who is later discarded and has to assimilate into society. The Kurt Russell-starring crime thriller *Dark Blue* (1992) plays against the backdrop of the Rodney King trial and riots.

He collaborated with Quentin Tarantino for the first time on *Death Proof* (2007) as Stuntman Mike. He played the character as a twisted version of John Wayne (Kurt Russell's father Bing had an uncredited role in *Rio Bravo* starring Wayne, who was one of Kurt's heroes since boyhood). Then, in Tarantino's *The Hateful Eight* (2015), Kurt starred as John "The Hangman" Ruth, a bounty hunter who, along with his bounty, finds himself in close quarters with some genuinely violent and unspeakable folk. The film had an impressive ensemble cast that included Samuel L. Jackson, Jennifer Jason Leigh, Walton Goggins, Demián Bichir, Tim Roth, Michael Madsen,

---

[8] *Todd McCarthy Variety (June 22, 1992)*

and Bruce Dern. He reunited with the director, working with him for a third time, on *Once Upon A Time in Hollywood* (2019). The film is a fairy tale tribute to the 1960s of Hollywood. Kurt narrates and plays the role of Randy Lloyd, a stunt coordinator in the film, which stars Leonardo DiCaprio as a Hollywood actor, and Brad Pitt as his charismatic stunt double.

For his role as Sheriff Franklin Hunt in S. Craig Zahler's macabre horror Western *Bone Tomahawk* (2015), the actor received praise. The film was also critically acclaimed. Additionally, Kurt took home the top acting honor at the *Fangoria* Chainsaw Awards. He also played Mr. Nobody, a recurring character in three entries in the *Fast and Furious* franchise. He also portrayed Ego in the Marvel movies *Guardians of the Galaxy Vol. 2* (2017) and *What If...?* (2021). He has also played Santa Claus in the films *The Christmas Chronicles* (2018) and *The Christmas Chronicles 2* (2020).

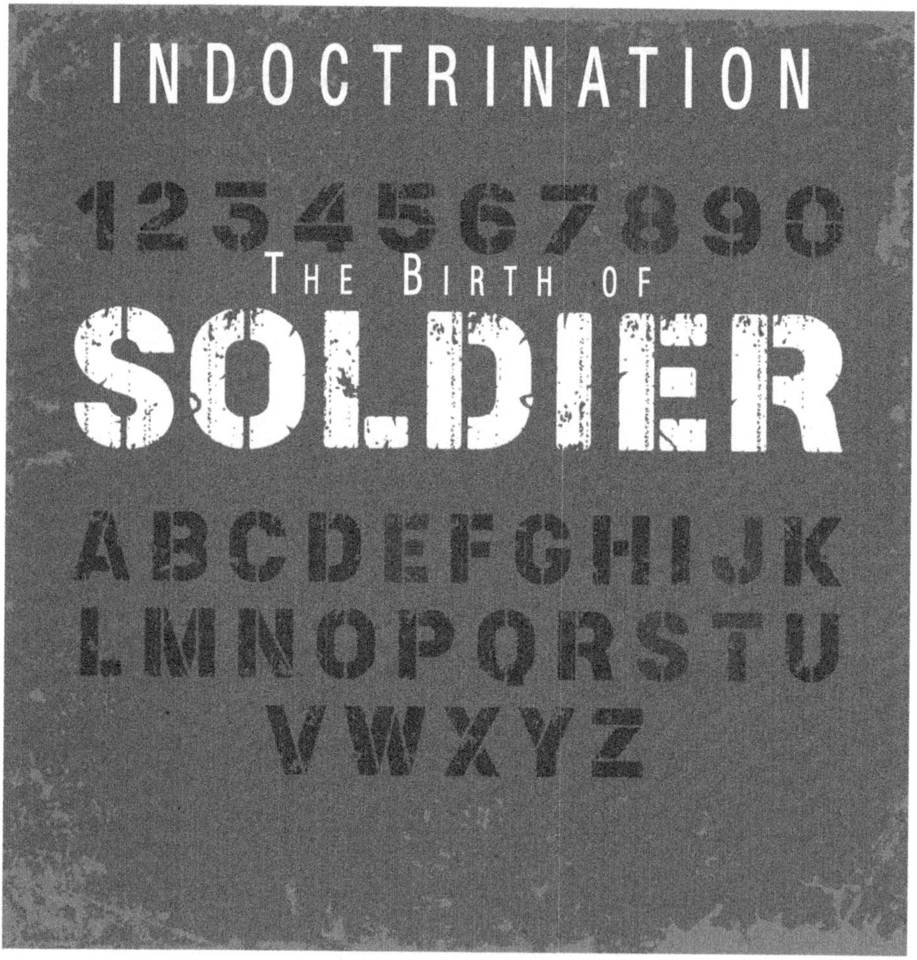
INDOCTRINATION
1234567890
THE BIRTH OF
SOLDIER
ABCDEFGHIJK
LMNOPQRSTU
VWXYZ

Indoctrination Definition - *the process of teaching a person or group to accept a set of beliefs uncritically.*

Soldier was written in 1984 by David Webb Peoples. It was an original screenplay that he conceived after seeing James Cameron's masterpiece *The Terminator*. Cameron's film had a tremendous influence on him and provided the inspiration for writing *Soldier*. The original script was very different from what eventually got on screen.

"I thought it was a fantastic script. Great characters—something I look for in all the films I do. Not just special effects and visual effects and all the stuff we put on the screen. The characters in this movie are characters you care about. It attracted my attention. It was a Western in space, written by David Webb Peoples, who wrote *Blade Runner* and *Unforgiven* among many other films. And I thought this was one of his best works." [9]—Jerry Weintraub "[*Soldier*] takes the narrative structure of *Shane*, but sets it on an alien planet. Rather than a gunfighter coming to a small town in the West, it's an old soldier who's been discarded by the military coming to a small town on a far flung planet. " [10]—Paul W.S. Anderson

"I found that the writing of Peoples provided a scenario that was very realistic, yet incredible. It was his writing style that drew me to this. It would be easy for other hands to make this sort of B-action picture. Instead, we have a classy look at a human being. And it was compelling to me in terms to play that character. It's almost pantomime. The guy just does not speak. He's someone who's never been asked an opinion. He's never been asked to think. He's always been simply told what to do...it's a little bit robotic, and yet underneath a mask, you realize at some point in the story when he just completely breaks down, that he's just a fractured human being." [11]—Kurt Russell

Many movies take their time getting to the screen. *Soldier* is no exception. It was born in 1984 as a script, and then released in 1998 as a movie. Picked for the lead role of the hardened veteran Sergeant Todd "3465" was

---

[9] *Cinefantastique Vol 20 No 9-10 November page 10 (1998)*

[10] *Cinefantastique Vol 20 No 9-10 November page 11 (1998)*

[11] *Cinefantastique Vol 20 No 9-10 November page 12 (1998)*

American actor Kurt Russell. He was 46 at the time, and it was the most physically challenging role of his career. Russell took off for a year to get into the mind and physicality of the character. He trained for three hours a day with trainer Greg Isaacs, who appears as one of the old soldiers in Todd's regiment in the film. Wyatt Russell played Todd as an 11-year-old. Jesse Littlejohn played the 8-year-old Todd in the opening scenes.

In the casting process, the producers chose against type when rounding up for the other lead roles: they selected Jason Scott Lee, who had previously played only heroes in films like Bruce Lee in the biographical movie *Dragon: The Bruce Lee Story* and Mowgli in *The Jungle Book*. In *Soldier*, he plays Caine 607. Gary Busey, famous for playing villains in films such as Mr. Joshua in *Lethal Weapon* and the sociopathic Peter Krill in *Under Siege*, was cast as Todd's captain, Church. Jason Isaacs plays Colonel Mekum. Later, Isaacs would land more military-type roles in Michael D. Steele in *Black Hawk Down* and Major Briggs in *Green Zone*. Their characters are bad guys; they represent the dehumanizing elements that have psychologically afflicted Todd all his life. At the time, Producer Jerry Weintraub described the film as a morality play pitting the human component of the soldiers against the march toward progress.

Connie Nielson, the actress who brought Sandra to life, was born in Denmark on July 3, 1965. Nielson started her acting career working alongside her mother. At 18, she travelled to France, working as an actress and model. In Italy, she went to drama school in Rome and studied master classes with Lydia Styx, a teacher at Piccolo di Milano in Milan. Connie lived in Italy for many years before moving to the United States in the 1990s. Before *Soldier*, she made her first big appearance in 1997 as Christabella Andreoli in the supernatural horror film *The Devil's Advocate*, starring Al Pacino and Keanu Reeves. Her *Soldier* character, Sandra, is a catalyst for Todd's spiritual awakening.

Sean Pertwee was born in England on June 4, 1964. He played Mace in *Soldier* and is best known for the role of Sgt. Wells in the horror film *Dog Soldiers*. He also played Inspector Lestrade in CBS's *Elmentary* and Alfred Pennyworth in Fox's *Gotham*. Pertwee had collaborated with director Paul W. S. Anderson and producer Jeremy Bolt previously on the 1994 crime film *Shopping* and the 1997 sci-fi horror *Event Horizon,* playing W.F. "Smitty" Smith, pilot of the Lewis and Clark.

Twins Jared & Taylor Thorne traded off playing Nathan, the son of Sandra and Mace. Portraying pioneer Jimmy Pig was actor Michael Chiklis, who was born on August 30, 1963 in Lowell, Massachusetts. His character plays an integral part in Todd's journey to rediscovering his lost humanity.

His nature also provides comic relief for the audience. Chiklis is known for his role as Los Angeles Police Department (LAPD) Detective Vic Mackey in the F.X. police drama *The Shield.* He won an Emmy Award for Lead Actor in a Drama Series in 2002, and was nominated again in 2003. He also played Commissioner Tony Scali on the ABC police drama *The Commish*, the Thing in two *Fantastic Four* films, and Jim Powell on the ABV sci-fi comedy-drama *No Ordinary Family.*

The rest of the cast were Mark Bringelson as Lieutenant Rubrick, K.K. Dodds as Lieutenant Sloan, James R. Black as Riley, Kyle Sullivan as Tommy, Corbin Bleu as Johnny, Sara Paxton as Angie, Jesse D. Goins as Chester, Mark De Alessandro as Goines, Vladimir Orlov as Romero, Carsten Norgaard as Green, Duffy Gaver as Chelsey, Brenda Wehle as Hawkins, Elizabeth Dennehy as Jimmy Pig's wife, Paul Dillon as Slade, Max Daniels as Red, Paul Sklar as Melton 249, Ellen Crawford as Ilona, Conni Marie Brazelton as Eva, Danny Turner as Omar, Elizabeth Huett as Janice, Jesse Littlejohn as Will, and the co-producer of the film, Jeremy Bolt, appeared in a cameo as an Enemy Soldier.

DAVID WEBB PEOPLES' FILMOGRAPHY

1973 *Steel Arena* (editor)

1976 *The Joy of Letting Go* (editor)

1977 *Who are the Debolts? (And Where Did They Get 19 Kids?)* (editor)

1980 *The Day After Trinity* (screenwriter, editor)

1982 *Blade Runner* (screenwriter)

1989 *Leviathan* (screenwriter, story)

1990 *The Blood of Heroes/Salute of the Jugger* (director, screenwriter)

1990 *Project: Alien* (screenwriter—credited as Anthony Able)

1992 *Hero* (co-story)

1992 *Unforgiven* (screenwriter)

1995 *Twelve Monkeys* (screenwriter)

1998 *Soldier* (screenwriter)

Peoples' View: An Interview with Screenwriter David Webb Peoples

Was it true that *Soldier* was initially titled *The Base* and had *First Blood*'s star, Sylvester Stallone, and director, Ted Kotcheff, attached at one point?

I've never heard of anything called *The Base*. I doubt if there was any, but I don't know that. What is true is that after the Geffen company bought the script, they brought Chuck Roven in as a producer. Then he brought Ted Kotcheff in as a director, so we worked for a little while together—Chuck, Ted Kotcheff, and me. I know nothing about any involvement with Stallone at all.

Was Clint Eastwood also interested in developing the project at one stage?

I don't know that either. Clint Eastwood said to me one time that he liked the script a lot, and I guess he thought about doing it. I don't know if he was ever involved beyond that, but he said he wasn't comfortable visualizing that world and didn't want to do it under those circumstances. He would have been very good, but that's the breaks.

Was it your intention that *Soldier* be a "side-quel" to *Blade Runner* (1982) and take place in the same universe?

No, I never had any thoughts about that.

Is it true that the premise of *Soldier* was based on an unused opening scene for *Blade Runner*, where a group of Replicants is dumped and left for dead on an off-world colony?

Well, that's not true, except I did write that scene for *Blade Runner*, the one that didn't get in right about the bodies dumped in a heap and so on.

That wonderful storyboard artist, Sherman Labby, did a beautiful picture of it. At any rate, that had nothing to do with *Soldier* other than the fact that I wrote that, you know. But one thing that I was always emphatic about with *Soldier* is it had nothing to do with genetic engineering. It was not genetic magic. It was all social engineering or training.

While *Blade Runner* was a film noir detective movie, *Soldier* is an old Hollywood-style Western. It uses the themes and tropes of Westerns. Did you always envision *Soldier* as a space Western transposing George Steven's 1953 Western *Shane*?

Ironically, it never crossed my mind until after I sold the script to the Geffen company. The executive there, Eric Eisner, said, wasn't it brilliant to write *Shane* in outer space. It never occurred to me, and he said that, but it was not in my mind when I was writing the screenplay.

Were there any scenes or material in *Soldier* you were disappointed to go from your original script?

I wrote *Soldier* in 1984. Very quickly on my own. I wrote it because I saw the first *Terminator* in the theater, stunned. And it was such a wonderful movie. I'd always wanted to write a movie in which there was a tough guy who would be seemingly unsympathetic in the lead, and I felt that the Terminator was almost there. Later in the sequel, it was determined he was the hero, but at the time, he was sort of a villain. But the fact is, he was so great. I went off, and I decided to write about this soldier.

While writing it, I had a kind of a vision. I thought about when you'd go to the zoo, in the old days—when the zoos had cages and everything—you'd go in there and see the tiger or the lion. But the Tigers were the beauties. You'd see the tiger pacing back and forth in the cage. Four hundred pounds of deadly stuff, just stalking back and forth. Who knows what he was thinking? And I imagined a little 18-month-old toddler slipping in the bars. And then everybody stared in amazement at this huge tiger. You had no idea what the tiger was thinking about, what he would do. He could just take a big bite, and the little kid would be gone. And the little kid is just a sweet, innocent pre-verbal 18-month-old, shuffling around, sweet as hell smiling at this strange big animal, not sensing any threat.

That, to me, was how *Soldier* was going to work for an audience. I wanted to do what I thought Jim Cameron had done when he raised *Terminator* above the genre. He made it a general audience picture; not just something for sci-fi nuts [but] something that was a real entertainment picture for everybody. And when I thought of this soldier, with this 18-month-old kid, and the audience holding its breath, never knowing what the soldier was going to do. The kid is just shuffling around, like, everything is fine. It was an image to me, and it created attention. I thought this would be magnificent in the movie. And I thought, the audience would love it. I would love it, the audience would love it, it would be great. And early in the production, I realized it wasn't going to happen. Now, there are good reasons not to shoot 18-month-old kids in the first place, and there are a lot of laws that let you only shoot a very short time a day with a little kid like that. And trying to get a performance out of a little kid at that age is tough. So, to do it would cost a lot of money, and you'd have to budget it, and it would be expensive, but like special effects, which also cost a lot of money. But you understand, hey, if I spend all this money on special effects, it's going to pay off because the audience will be delighted. Nobody got the idea here that the 18-month-old kid would be as exciting and powerful for the audience as special effects. Would be. This is, of course, way before all the current CGI techniques, but at any rate. So they were going to do it with a kid who now, again, imagine the difference in *The Godfather*. When the Godfather is in the garden, and he dies, and there's that little pre-verbal kid running around innocently. Imagine if that was a six-year-old or something. What a difference. So, when I realized, they weren't going to cast an 18-month-old kid, I was extremely disappointed. And I thought, well, this isn't going to be the movie I dreamed of. And I'll bet it doesn't succeed commercially. And I'm disappointed.

I did write a draft with an older kid, and I did what I was told. But I was just so discouraged at the thought of that. And, and I love the script so much. And several things happened that made me think, you know, if I watch that movie, it will break my heart. I'd love to see Kurt Russell, and everybody says he's terrific in it. And I loved him as an actor, always. He's a magnificent actor. And so, when people tell me he's great, as Todd, I think jeez, I'd like to see that. But at the same time, this script was so important and meant so much to me, and I can't believe that I just won't break my heart to see the movie. So far, I haven't seen the movie.

Two additional scenes were not as important. One of the scenes was when you write an anti-hero like Todd, like Travis Bickle, like Dirty Harry, you need to challenge the audience. And you need to say to the audience, hey, I dare you to like this guy. So, I had written a very brief scene, like a quarter of a page, in which a bunch of soldiers is massacring the family in a hut. And you can see Todd in the group of soldiers, although he's not the one doing the actual shooting. And that's what soldiers do. They're involved in these horrible incidents that destroy their heads and all that stuff. So, I thought it was a powerful scene. And it was very short, very little. And it wouldn't have cost a lot to shoot it. And I thought, and I understood, that you could screen the film, and maybe that would be too much. And maybe the audience would never be able to sympathize with Todd after that, in which case, you'd have to cut that scene out. But I hoped that they would shoot it. It would be in the previews, which would not repel the audience. They would be shocked and challenged, but they would not be repelled. So that, I knew, was coming out, and that disappointed me [but] it wasn't the end of the world. And then the other thing I wrote was one of the most beautiful scenes I think I've ever written and one of the more imaginative ones. And I saw some dailies at one point, and saw that nobody had understood the scene and then just gone away to something else. And I felt very bad about that. And so, again, I anticipate great disappointment if I watched it despite how good Kurt Russell would be.

It's funny because a lot of your writing, your scripts your ideas, have struck a chord, especially in these times they are very relevant. *Twelve Monkeys* are so relevant with what's going on.

It's like we knew something. [Laughs]

In *Soldier*, Todd 3465 (played by Kurt Russell) is pitted against a new breed of soldiers. An implication in the film is that the genetically engineered soldiers meant to replace Todd and his fellow soldiers are, in fact, replicants. Is this true, and are they Nexus-9 replicants?

That was never my intention. My intention was always that the soldiers were done by more natural means. Nowadays, if you follow MMA, and you see all the different drugs that can help you [with] in MMA, which you're not allowed to do—there are all sorts of things people do with our bodies to make them more lethal. And I was thinking in those terms, not in terms of genetics. If you were a military person who wanted to make soldiers more deadly and more like fighting machines, you would explore all sorts of things, quite apart from genetics. That's a whole other thing. Yes, you could do genetic engineering. But there are other things. In World War II, the German soldiers were issued methamphetamines, and the plan was to keep them fighting for long periods. And in fact, they did do some remarkable stuff that shocked the Russians. When the Germans just didn't stop marching, and they were credited to meth, and so on. Now I'm assuming that if these were military people, they would treat each soldier as a valuable thing and wouldn't want to kill him with too much stuff or bad stuff that would harm him. But they would want to figure out ways to adjust and make it work that the soldier would perform to the max.

Was it purposeful that Todd bears similarities to both Roy Batty, the deadly android of *Blade Runner* who is condemned in the end by his obsolescence, and the retired gunslinger of *Unforgiven*, Munny? The quote "It's a hell of a thing killing a man. You take away all he's got and all he's ever gonna have" comes to mind. The characters both must use violence in the end.

Well, I have to say characters like that influenced me. I was enormously influenced if you've ever seen Henry King's *The Gunfighter* (1950) starring Gregory Peck. I remembered loving it when I was 10 years old. Still, I didn't realize how much it had influenced me until I saw it many years later after *Unforgiven* came out as a very powerful film. I also was a great fan of reading Dostoevsky, and, at any rate, Dostoevsky's people, his heroes, are all very flawed and troubled, and so on, and somehow that influenced me. So, I related to that kind of character. You know, I wish I invented Walter White and Tony Soprano. Still, at any rate, troubled characters are something I relate to, so I think that sort of comes out when I write. But I certainly don't think or intend to make any similarities.

***Taxi Driver* just had its anniversary. I know that inspired you.**

That's one of the most important films to me. That film was hugely influential on me. I had started writing screenplays, and I wasn't willing to have anybody killed in my screenplays because I thought deaths in Hollywood movies were so phony and everything, and I just didn't want to do it. I didn't think death was a joke, and they do that, you know, in some Hollywood movies and so on. They do it in James's Bond, and it's okay. I like James Bond pictures, but I could never write anything like that. Then I saw *Taxi Driver*, and that just knocked my socks off the same way *Terminator* did. Paul Schrader's Travis Bickle is a guy. Paul dares you to be sympathetic to that guy. And that, to me, is one of the most important movies in my personal development. I began to write *Unforgiven* shortly after that, not immediately but a few years after it, and everything it just opened up the door to me that you didn't have to have people shoot each other and then have tea the next hour or something like that. You could actually write about people and just make a very important film.

What kind of themes were you exploring with the script?

I must tell you. I must be very clear about this. I don't think about themes when I write. Now, if I look at the script, I will say that the theme is violence, or when's violence good, when's violence bad? Is there any solution, etc? I'd say that would be a theme. But I didn't think of it that way. Not too long ago, somebody sent me a book about screenplay writing that articulated my own perfectly. It seemed particularly relevant to me; it described me in the way I write perfectly. And I know other writers write like me. I know other writers write differently, but this book says, "The experienced dramatist or screenwriter seldom begins with a theme, or attempts to fashion a story in order to present a philosophical position, which might be called a thesis. This method leads to cliches, propaganda, and lifeless characters, because all the human issues of the drama have been subordinated to this thesis the author is out to prove. Instead, an accomplished screenwriter creates characters and situations, and then chooses a culmination and resolution that seems right and satisfactory to his own feelings about the subject matter. In other words, a good screenwriter lets the theme take care of itself. The theme thus becomes not some point to be proven, but the subject matter itself, that aspect of human existence, this story will explore." Now that quote is from David Howard and Edward Mabley's *The Tools of Screenwriting: A Writer's Guide to the Craft and Elements of a Screenplay* and is something I had never read before. But it so perfectly describes the way I work, which is to not think about a theme or a thesis or anything but to think about a story and a character. And out of the story and the character, there may come a theme, or there may come a thesis. I don't know. I don't try to force it in there. It's simply what's going on in this story, and the only thing I can say is I deliberately go for ambiguous things. For example, is violence good? Or is violence bad? I would not want to write a script to prove violence was good, and I would not want to prove violence was bad. It's an ongoing question, so I don't want to try and answer it. I'm not interested in answering it. That's not what I do. I think it's part of our human nature, and I said that's what I like about Scorsese's films because, at least in his early films, it was always the idea that violence was part of the human condition. That violence wasn't good. It wasn't bad. It was what we all had inside ourselves and how it came out was how it came out.

You'd prefer the audience to interpret their view on it?

I'm not interested in drawing conclusions. I'm interested in the characters. I'm interested in stories. I like stories. And stories don't always prove something, or if they do prove something, it's not necessarily the author's intention that they prove something. So that's just my general [approach], and whenever I've tried to do it the other way, like this quote said, everything comes out forced, and it sounds like it's a plan or something. It doesn't sound like characters. It sounds like characters saying what the writer wants them to say, so he can prove their point. And good writing is when the characters surprise you and say things you didn't expect them to say.

You like Scorsese's early work. How about people like Oliver Stone or Kubrick, those kinds of filmmakers?

Kubrick, he's a very cerebral filmmaker, and I'm not a bit like him, which doesn't mean I can't appreciate his work. His work is sometimes very good and sometimes not so great. I love his earlier pictures, like *The Killing* and *Paths of Glory*, more than I liked his later pictures, but I like many of his pictures anyway. And it's just that he has a different sensibility and thinks differently. And I don't think that way. So that's all I can say to that. When you look at a script by Oliver Stone, like, *Midnight Express*, that's a wonderful character story. Now, I know he took it from a true story, but the bottom line is the characters dominate that story. It's not like a message or anything like that dominates. It is a guy who gets into trouble, and we get to meet him and see how he reacts to his situation, and it's very exciting and very good. And I don't see that as plotted out. And normally, Oliver Stone stays away from plotted out when he's at his best.

If you look at human history, we are constantly at war. While some scholars see war as a universal and ancestral aspect of human nature, others argue it results from specific socio-cultural, economic, or ecological circumstances. Like in every war, the character of Todd has become a psychiatric casualty of war as a consequence of the stresses of military life. He begins suffering from post-traumatic stress. Was this an important issue to you? What were you pushing towards? Did you know of anyone in the Army who had fought in combat when you were writing the script?

I did know some people, but I didn't draw on their experiences. I was aware that when I go to the grocery store, I may be dealing with a checker who's been in combat and killed people and all that, and he is just a nice guy and just a normal person. I do have a communication with a man who has PTSD, so I'm aware of those things. But I wasn't trying to write about those things.

In my view on war, the answers to the business of socio-economic and all that stuff are true, but they're superficial. Fundamentally, we have wars because we're animals, and as animals, we have the kind of territorial needs that other animals have. We can discuss them, which I don't think lions can discuss their territorial needs, but they are primitive impulses, and sometimes we try to master them in different ways. But fundamentally, we are animals in that we're condemned to being animals, and all we can do is modify our behaviour to the best of our ability. So, to me, that's where wars come from; they come from our animal nature.

Many people see human beings as creatures dominated by reason, but that's not the case at all. We do have the ability to use reason. But we are not dominated by reason, right? We could well decide that sex was a bad idea, [but that] doesn't make any difference. We're still going to be sexually aroused very much of the time. We don't have choices in a lot of these things. We have some choices in how we behave. But fundamentally, our needs are animal needs. So, in the story that we see there, we see these pacifists have modified their animal, their need for war, and they don't think they need war. And then, suddenly, somebody comes in and is taking over their place. Well, Jesus, now they've got a problem, and this is all the circumstances and everything that comes of all this weird stuff.

When you wrote *Soldier*, you'd seen *Terminator*. Then, seven years later, you had *Terminator 2: Judgment Day*, which completely flipped the coin in the sense that you had the Terminator, who was the ultimate villain, the ultimate killing machine, and he changed into a good guy. So, the moral compass was flipped. With the character of *Soldier*, I'm guessing that it was intact in your original script with the baby, and I'm guessing that it's kind of like what you did with the character of Todd. He starts as the ultimate killing machine; you're terrified of him because you don't know what he will do, and it's like the Terminator in *T2*. By the end of the story, he learns the value of human life.

Yeah, okay, but *learns* is a strong word here. He realizes, perhaps. He senses the value. He's not a thinker. He's not going, "I think now that human life has value." He doesn't do that. Now he realizes his awareness has been raised, so he has a different point of view. He's been treated in different circumstances, and when we see him, he first becomes a soldier. He was 18 months old, and he hadn't formed at all. And now he's had a chance to form a little bit on a more human basis, and so on.

What's your favourite memory or memories of working on the movie?

I guess my favourite memory was Paul Anderson bringing me with him to meet Kurt Russell, which was thrilling because I'm a huge Kurt Russell fan. I mean, he was Snake Plissken, and he was in that picture with Meryl Streep, *Silkwood*, and he has been in all sorts of pictures, and he is always terrific, and that was thrilling to meet him. I saw *Bone Tomahawk* recently. He was wonderful in it.

What do you think of the movie personally?

I've never seen it. I don't have anything against it. People tell me they like it. So, I guess it's pretty good. It's just it isn't what I envisioned, and what I envisioned was such a powerful hit that people would have asked me about it a lot. But it wasn't to happen, and I think the studio just didn't get it. When you write, it's one of those things; some people must get it. And here, they just saw expense. They didn't see the reward. They saw risk and no reward.

FILMING
1234567890
SOLDIER
ABCDEFGHIJK
LMNOPQRSTU
VWXYZ

"The idea of men being dehumanized by war is a classic idea" says Director Paul W.S. Anderson during a break in filming. "*Soldier* is science fiction, but it could easily be about Vietnam, World War II, or the Boer War. It really has that timeless feel to it." [12]

Interview with Fred Fontana Associate Producer

Soldier was a very big part of my life for about two-and-a-half years. The prep, with all the visual effects and practical set build, took a very long time. The script had been around the studio for quite awhile. When it finally went forward with us, it was a huge undertaking as you can imagine. There were several actors considered to play the lead, including discussions involving Arnold Schwarzenegger, Sylvester Stallone, and we even had Keanu Reeves at one point. But it was finally locked in with Kurt Russell, who to this day is probably the most professional actor I've ever worked with. Such a tremendous star that gave his all for this role, and the discipline he undertook to stay so physically fit was impressive. He was a true pleasure.

We had a lot of great actors in *Soldier* including Jason Scott Lee, Connie Nielsen, Jason Isaacs, Gary Busey and Michael Chiklis. The cast was fantastic and all were wonderful to work with.

I have such an emotional attachment to *Soldier* because of all the hard work we all put in on this film—especially Paul Anderson, the director. But sadly, the film came and went without much fanfare. I don't know if the studio didn't believe in it or what really happened, but to this day, people see it on television and remark what a good film it was and always ask, "When did this come out? I never heard about it."

We shot the bulk of *Soldier* on Stage 16 at Warner Bros. Stage 16 is the largest stage on the studio lot, and we built—led by David Snyder our Production Designer—one of the most impressive sets I've ever seen. The entire village where Kurt's character (Todd) lived was built on that stage. We

[12] *Starlog Magazine, Issue 256 page 33 (1998)*

had more fun just walking around the set, up in the catwalks, getting lost in the trails of the village. It was incredible. In fact, people that had nothing to do with the film kept wanting to come by the stage for a tour of the set—including a lot of the stars who were filming various shows on the lot at the time. I remember Clint Eastwood visiting. George Clooney came by. A couple of the cast members from *Friends*. It was great to make the movie in Los Angeles. We almost did it in Australia (which I'm sure would have been amazing, by the way). But shooting in LA was so nice after having done so many pictures on location. It was nice to stay home for once! Besides the Warner Bros stages, we also shot in Downtown LA, the Santa Monica airport hangar, and in a desolate quarry out in Irwindale. But the bulk of the film was done on stage.

Soldier was not my first film at Warner Bros. I joined Jerry Weintraub's producing team around 1990-1991, and it was a big thrill to work with such a legendary movie guy as Jerry. Just listening to Weintraub relive his long and formidable career was any filmmaker's dream, and to listen to him tell his stories over the many years was an experience I'll never forget. He was a true mentor. The first movie I did with him was *Pure Country* that starred George Strait, Isabel Glasser, Lesley Ann Warren, and Kyle Chandler. We shot that film on location in Texas and had such an incredible time there. It was my indoctrination into the Weintraub world, which would be my life for the next decade or so.

Though we had been working on *Soldier* for quite awhile already, the first day of full crew prep was officially Monday, October 13, 1997. It was a bit of a sad day for all of us associated with Jerry. John Denver passed away the day before in the glider crash, and it was certainly a huge shock to Jerry as the two had worked so closely together for so many years; not just with John's music, but Jerry produced *Oh God!*, which John starred in. So we got off to a bumpy start that day nonetheless. But we were excited to begin this new adventure. We worked a long time prepping "Soldier" for cameras, probably the longest prep time on any movie I have ever made in my career. It was an arduous prep as there was so much to deal with; a large cast, tons of wardrobe fittings, camera tests with the green screens, final touch up on the sets. Sets on three stages. Makeup tests. Prop approvals. Second-unit planning. That process alone was exhausting.

We finally started filming on Tuesday, January 20th, 1998. It was a fabulous day. The first shot was an establishing shot of when Kurt Russell (Todd) arrives at the Pandora village. It was a breathtaking shot, impressive in its artistry and epic, even if it was done on stage! The ride had officially begun.

One of my clearest memories on set from *Soldier* was one of the days we filmed with the green mamba snake (one of the top five deadliest snakes in the world, I believe). We did not use a fake. It was real, and the set was pretty intense that day. Of course, the snake's mouth was sutured so it couldn't bite, but it was still poisonous. In the scene, the snake had to crawl up the bed that Sean Pertwee and Connie Nielsen were asleep in. If you look closely, you can see the actor's neck pulsating a bit as the snake got closer and closer to their faces. Personally, I don't like snakes, so I was feeling just as nervous as they were. Eventually, when the film was finished, it was decided by the studio that they wanted to add more snakes. So one day in post-production, we did some reshooting to add more snakes into the film. We were back on Stage 16 and using a double for Kurt (he was already off making another movie), and we brought in 150 snakes of all kinds to the set to get a few seconds of "Todd" dealing with scattering snakes. There I stood on set, inches away from countless snakes. When "action" was called, the snakes were dumped out onto the floor of the set, and within seconds, slithered away in all directions, including one that decided to slither up my leg. Will never forget that. The fun part for the wranglers were gathering them all up once the shot was completed. Legend has it that not every snake was accounted for when we were done! So who knows? Someday there might be a 25-foot mamba snake slithering around Stage 16! Doubtful, though, because as soon as we were done, *Perfect Storm* moved into that stage, and the tank was filled with water for the ocean scenes! The Snake scene was shot by Oliver Wood.

Soldier was a 75-day shoot. We started shooting in January of 1998. It was a grueling shoot. We had nights. Second unit. Long days. So much CGI and green screen work. It's interesting, we were cutting edge back then, and yet today it would have taken much less time and certainly not as much money to pull off what we did back then. Technology has come a long way from 1998! Wc also had to deal with an injury to Kurt Russell, who hurt his leg doing a stunt on the show on Stage 16. We had to shut down a couple days and rework the schedule to accommodate Kurt's healing time. But he was such a trooper and readied himself as quickly as possible. In fact, the scenes of him running (in Downtown LA) were shot while he was still recuperating. Kurt was a team player of the highest regard. He was always on time. Knew his lines (funny, thoughm that he had so few words to say). And he worked out constantly on set to keep that physique.

I am very proud of *Soldier* and truly don't think it was given a proper chance to be successful. In the days before streaming and when films still played in the theaters, no one even knew *Soldier* was out. I remember opening weekend, and when the numbers came in on Monday and we just floundered, it was depressing. We had all worked so hard to make the best movie possible—one we were all very happy with. It was sad that the audiences didn't flock to it. Kurt is very good in the film and the supporting cast were top notch. I think the themes in the film are very relevant today. I loved that we had set pieces and props from the original *Blade Runner* incorporated into the set design (thankfully done and brilliantly executed by David Snyder). Some of my favourite times personally were working so closely with Jeremy Bolt (Paul Anderson's producing partner). Overall, I think even though it wasn't an immediate financial success for the studio, it was a film that spoke to a specific audience and tapped into the sci-fi world with enough interest that the film became a very solid performer on television. That is where so many people finally got to see it (thank you FX, where it ran for several years) and would reach out and compliment the hard work and say how much they liked it. So many years after its release, I think it was finally getting its due. It's a good film, and I am thankful for having been such a part of it. When you spend several years of your life working on just one movie, it's fulfilling to know that people respond to it. I'd say it's become a cult classic, which is fantastic after all these years.

I just recently produced and co-wrote a new animated TV series called *Road of Vengeance*, which will make its debut later in 2022. The nice part of that show was recasting and reuniting with Jason Scott Lee, who voices a major character in the series. We had not seen each other in well over a decade, but we were able to reconnect on *Road* and reminisce a bit about our days running around the Warner Bros lot making a film we both truly enjoyed being a part of. That's the thing about making movies in general—they are never easy, they are always a ton of hard, excruciating work, but you are forever bonded with the team that lived it together. Forever.

Interview with Allen D. Easton Camera Operator: "A" Camera

How did you end up being a camera operator for *Soldier*?

I did *Mortal Kombat* with Paul Anderson, and then he invited me to do *Soldier*, which is where I met David Tattersall and had a great time on the show. I thought all our actors, everybody worked hard. Our lead actor is Kurt Russell. If you see that movie, he's all bulked up, and he worked hard getting himself in shape before we started production, and it showed on the film.

What kind of challenges did this movie provide you, and which were the hardest, most enjoyable, funniest, and satisfying scenes or sequences to work behind?

Boy, you know, you were taking me back many years ago. I think we shot that movie in '97, and it came out in '98. I tell you that a lot of it has been a lot of shows under the belt since then. It was an outstanding experience. Having worked with Paul Anderson already, he knows me knowing sort of what he likes visually. I was able to offer up a lot of advice. For a lot of ideas, as we were designing each shot or a scene would progress, working with David Tattersall was incredibly talented. But Paul also allowed me the freedom to give ideas and suggestions, so I was very much involved in the contribution of coverage ideas and shot design. It made my experience much better. So, because again, I was able to contribute, Paul made all the difference because we had such a good working relationship on *Mortal Kombat* that allowed that communication to get even better. After all, he had great trust in what I was doing and my ideas to help move the whole storyline along.

How long did it take to shoot the movie?

It seems to me it was around two-and-a-half months of production. There was quite a bit of the second unit where I wasn't involved. I was involved with mostly all the principal photography, with Kurt and the main actors there. I remember the last weeks of the movie, where the end of the film takes place with that whole fight scene in the rain [was] mostly handheld. That part of it was pretty physical because it rained and rained, and we had days of rain outside. We shot that, as I recall, in the summer. So we go out to Burbank. It could be 100 degrees outside, and I'd be soaking wet even with all the rain gear. We take our rain gear, hang it out in the sun during lunch, be nice and dry, and then immediately we'd be back in the rain. It was easier to shoot it handheld, to move around, and stay up with them. Also, we did the same thing with Paul on *Mortal Kombat*, being close in with wide lenses to bring the action and make the audience feel like you're right there in the fighting seat, rather than being farther back on a longer lens. That way, the audience can feel that closeness of the hits and the sweat and everything else in the water coming off the lands and off of them.

The final fight in the film is better than many of the fight sequences staged today. It felt natural. It was just two people going at it.

Right. I got a few bumps and bruises as the fight scene continued, just because we were in such proximity. And, of course, a lot of that was a stunt coordinator working with Paul working with the actors ahead of time, knowing that Paul liked this close interaction with them and being intimate.

What were your favourite memories of working on the film?

Kurt Russell was the ultimate professional while we were making the film. He was always ready. We weren't waiting, and there wasn't any problem getting him out of the trailer. He was on the set, ready to go. He knew what was going on. I found that if I needed something or had a suggestion, he would listen. And if it worked well for him, we would do it. But also, it was necessary. He also understood that I'm the audience when we're filming. The audience is not the people over on the side watching him. It's not the director off in the corner. It's what the cameras capture, and I'm the camera at that point. S,o I want to make sure that I get the best from him for whatever angles and position and performance and make sure that the cameras are capturing it.

The worst thing you want is to be sitting in dailies the next day and something comes up on the screen, and there's a boom mic in the shot. There's an Apple box sitting in the corner, and there's a light stand that I missed. And they don't look to anybody else, they look at me. They all turn and go, "How come you didn't see that? Why didn't you catch that?" So the responsibility, even though nowadays, it's changed dramatically, because everybody has a monitor on the step. Everybody is looking at a monitor, and you know video village has become the big word, where there are ten people in video village watching, nowadays, so we finished a shot. And nobody even asked me how anything was because everybody was watching it.

A lot of times, people make decisions based on the monitor. And sometimes they don't understand what's happening around the camera, and around the actors that for whatever decision or things that didn't work, or it did work. But that's just the way the world has become, in the sense of filming. In my early days, before video monitors were so prominent on the set, the director would sit next to me, sit under the camera and sit beside the camera. And so, he was part of that feeling that was happening right there. And on the set, rather than being 30 feet away, inside a tent. And it's a different feeling. You're looking. It's you and I looking at a monitor right now. And you're trying to get the sense of everything around me. But all you see is right there. But when you're on the set, you see all of this information coming in, and I feel it gives the director and the actors a better chance of feeling the performance. But I've become that minority these days because it's the way of the world. You know, they'll be looking at three cameras simultaneously. They'll have three monitors set up, and they're watching all three monitors. And I feel it takes away, to a certain extent.

I guess you get with people like Spielberg and Scorsese and even Paul, they're more intent on what's happening with one camera, or what's happening on the set, rather than just looking at the monitor and thinking about the cuts all the time. But it's very much a different world. And also, the use of the camera has come a long way; Steadicam has made filmmaking a whole new world [in terms of] what you can do with it. In the sense of not needing Dolly tracks or a dolly, I mean, just reading what the director can have the camera do has changed it. And it probably is better in a lot of ways.

What did you think of the movie when you saw it, and what was your reaction?

There should have been maybe a little more dialogue with Kurt for people to understand more about the movie. Visually, for me, I thought it was great. Paul Anderson is huge about visual storytelling. The criticism I heard was that the guy didn't say anything the whole movie. I don't know if people understood that. And indeed, sitting in a movie theatre, people did not get it. I had a great time and when we built that set that they made on stage 16 at Warner Brothers. I remember one of the shots that scared the daylights out of me, they put me in, basically, in a boson's chair at the top of the junk planet, And they flew me across the whole stage and dropped me down as we were approaching into the main set with a handheld camera.

It was one giant planet. I'm flying across the stage as I descend with the handheld camera going into the perspective of either the ship or somebody's concept of going into it. The shot, I guess, came out great. I'm not as great on heights, significantly dropping me down with the camera, but the shot worked out. It was fun, but I don't think the audience understood the movie.

Interview with Dennis Maguire First Assistant Director

How did you end up being the first assistant director?

I am third generation film, and my father had been an Assistant Director early in his career. I was on many film sets growing up and knew I wanted to make movies at a young age. I started working on films,. I worked on *All the President's Men* as a prop-maker, building sets. Six years later, I had the opportunity to work as a set P.A. on a film called *Only When I Laugh*. I was building sets on that film and asked if I could interview as a set P.A., and was granted the job. I did my 400 days as a set P.A. on films and petitioned the DGA (Directors Guild of America) to let me join as a Second Assistant Director. I was accepted.

How did you get the assignment to be the First A.D. for Soldier?

I was asked to have an interview with Paul Anderson by the producer of the film, Jerry Weintraub. I had worked on two other films by Jerry, and it worked out with Paul to become his First Assistant Director. Working for

Paul, it was evident that he would be a successful director, which came to fruition.

How long did you work on the production, and which scenes did you work on?

In a large gravel mine pit, the large Exterior Spaceship Ribcage Set was built in Azuza, California. We had about 12 weeks of prep, and I think it was a 74-Day shoot in Los Angeles. Mostly on Stage at Warner Bros. Studios in Burbank, California.

How was the experience working with the cast and crew? What happened behind the scenes?

Our cast was fantastic. Kurt Russell set the tone by being a great guy and a true professional actor. He was incredibly generous to the twin boys, who were hired to play the child in the film. They were great, but Kurt and I both would help Paul Anderson out with them, because Kurt knew all about working as a child actor, and I had children, which Paul Anderson did not. Connie Neilson was amiable and a total pro. I appreciated Jason Issacs, too. I have experienced many British Actors in my career, having worked in London on *Patriot Games*, *Evita*, and *Speed.* I am a massive fan of British actors' work ethics and their love of the work.

The crew was very professional, and there it came from working with our British DP, David Tattersall, an incredibly kind gentleman and an impressive D.P. His attitude was always upbeat, no matter the situation. His camera, grip, and electrical crew were fantastic and hard working. We had a tight schedule, and we met it.

How was it working onset of the Arcadia 237 planet, and were there any obstacles to overcome?

The set was a one-acre set inside Stage 16 at Warner Bros. Our production designer was the art director on *Blade Runner*. It was three or four levels high. There was a full-size DC-3 airplane inside the set, and a bullet train. We did have a studio safety meeting regarding the set, and all parties worked to keep the cast and crew safe over the issues raised. My staff were excellent and always conscientious of whom we would ask to work on the various levels to maintain the safety and security of cast and crew. We did some colossal action pieces inside that stage and set.

Mainly the cable camera shot from one corner of the stage/set to the meeting house doors. We had multiple stunts happening on various levels at the same time, too. But I knew my stunt team very well, led by David Ellis and Dick Ziker. Two of Hollywood's legends. The special-effects team was the best, and I knew some of them from previous films. They were always on it. I hurt my knee working on this film. I tore my medial meniscus while climbing up to shoot the chain fight between Jason and Kurt one day. That set was built in a hangar in Santa Monica, and yes, at times, we were 30 feet off the ground fighting and shooting it.

Additional memories:

I was the one that brought in a friend of mine to photograph Kurt Russell to photoshop different crew cuts/hairstyles on him. Back then, photoshop was new. It allowed the director, Jerry Weintraub, Kurt, and the studio execs to weigh in. Kurt wanted to shave his head. Eventually, the crew cut won out. And I believe they had my friend photoshop the tattoo in different locations and sizes. My friend that helped is Chuck Hawekotte. Jerry Weintraub was quite surprised by photoshop at the time. Kurt was pushing for the shaved head look, and of course, no one wanted to cut his hair to see it. So the 360 still shots were stitched together, and Chuck was able to show everyone the different hairstyles without cutting and wig fittings.

What do you think of the movie personally?

Kurt's role was initially Sylvester Stallone. We were to make this film immediately after *The Specialist*, but Sly took another film, and Kurt was cast instead. Although I am not mainly a sci-fi filmgoer, I did enjoy the film as a movie-going experience.

Interview with Andy Spilkoman Second second Assistant Director

How did you get the assignment to be the second second AD for Soldier?

I was friends with Dennis Maguire, so Dennis hired me to work for him on *Soldier*.

How long did you work on the production, and which scenes did you work on?

I worked on the entire shoot. It was 70-80 days, and I am sure I have some of the paperwork somewhere. I worked on all the scenes and all the sets. I have a photo of myself wader-deep in the water for the scene where Todd pops up out of the water and kills the new soldiers.

How was the experience working with the cast and crew, and what happened behind the scenes?

Kurt Russell is one of the nicest people I have ever worked with. This includes any job I have ever had in this industry and others I worked in before movies and TV. Kurt's son, Wyatt, was the boy carrying the flag in the scene where the boy that lagged behind was shot; Wyatt was the best behaved of all the other kids, in my opinion; a testament to Kurt and Goldie as excellent parents and human beings. Gary Busey is a very interesting man. I enjoyed asking him questions I am sure were never asked of him. Gary and I were talking about *Big Wednesday* and *The Buddy Holly Story*. Gary told me they dyed his hair black, and he was Buddy Holly. Then they made it blonde again, and he was in *Big Wednesday*.

I had nice conversations with Michael Chiklis, we talked about the show he was in called *The Commish*, and how he was 26 playing 40, and we talked about *Wired* and him playing John Belushi. Later in my career, I worked with Jim Belushi, and we had a conversation about the day his brother John died. I would go on to work with Michael Chiklis again on *The Shield*.

How was it working onset of the Arcadia 237 planet? Were there any obstacles to overcome?

The main set was built on Stage 16 at Warner Bros., the tallest stage in Hollywood, with a very deep pit. The floor can be removed. This gives the set designers time to construct a multi-layered set. The set on stage was very elaborate. The explosions were all practical, as were the fires. The FX crew constantly painted rubber cement on the sets and set them ablaze. A fire extinguisher put the flames out. The big scenes with the crawlers were shot in a gravel pit in Irwindale, Ca. We had giant wind machines mounted onto 48-foot flat trailers. I recall being told they were from the movie *Twister*; Vermiculite, a mineral used in planting, was blown into the exterior set with the wind machines; this was uncomfortable as it got into everything; hair and clothes.

I was the AD on a splinter unit, and we shot scenes of the 50-calibre machine guns firing from the top of the crawler as it was driving. That was fun. The fight scene between Caine and Todd was filmed on Warner Bros. Stage 16. That scene took over a week to film. We made it rain on the stage every day after lunch. It was my turn to run the set, inside a stage, in my rain gear, with a soaking wet rolling camera.

What do you think of the movie personally?

I just re-watched the movie via Amazon (I invested $2.99), and I saw the movie in 1998 when it came out. I was not impressed then, but today I liked it. It brought back many memories of making the film. This was not an easy film to make.

Interview with Jayson Merrill Key Second Assistant Director

How did you end up being a key second assistant director?

I replaced the second AD on *The Postman* and apparently did a good enough job for Dennis Maguire to hire me as his key second AD on the next one. *Soldier* was my first job as a key second AD.

How long did you work on the production for, and which scenes did you work on?

I worked on the main unit, so I was there for all scenes other than what second unit (action unit) shot.

How was the experience working with the cast and crew, and what went on behind the scenes?

The experience was great with the crew. Jerry Weintraub was a true professional and had a big personality. Susan Ekins was a delight to work with. Very nice and approachable. Paul Anderson was really good at his craft and a delight to work with. The cast was great. I was super excited to work with Kurt Russell because I've known him since I was eight-years-old. He's as good as it gets when dealing with cast. Jason Lee was a hard worker and great to work with. Gary Busey could be a handful at times, but overall, he was fun to work with. Just had to get him there. Connie Nielsen was a sweetheart.

Behind the scenes, we had a legendary cast and crew golf tournament. My team consisted of Kurt Russell, Oliver Hudson, Jim Van Wyck, and myself. We were the first off and came in with a score of 14 under. That last group that came in claimed to be 14 under, so we had a playoff. After three margaritas, we went to the first tee and got after it. We had all tournament members follow us the whole way from the first tee, up the fairway and surround the green. At one point, the marshall came out and threatened to call the sheriff, and of course, Busey or Jason Isaac let him have it. Jim Van Wyck was the last to putt and drained it for the win. Everyone went nuts. Most clutch putt I've ever witnessed. The sheriff never came. I found out years later the other team cheated to get to 14 under. Our score was legit.

How was it working onset of the Arcadia 237 planet, and were there many obstacles to overcome?

There's always obstacles to overcome on a movie set. I think at the time it was the biggest set ever constructed on stage at Warner Bros. We also filmed in a rock quarry in Azusa CA. The community was on stage and the outskirts were shot in the rock quarry. Lots of dust and gunfire. Those giant military assault vehicles were made from massive dump trucks. The art department designed a shell to put around them. They had twin 50-caliber guns on top that we'd load with 100's of rounds in each. They'd get the cue to fire and start shooting the rounds, but we'd yell cut and they'd unload until they were done because they couldn't hear a thing.

What do you think of the movie personally?

At first, I didn't think much of the movie, maybe because I knew the story so well. But as I watched it years after, I seemed to enjoy it more. It's always fun to look back and reminisce at what it took to make it and all the friends I made along the way.

Interview with Phil Shanahan Second Assistant Camera

How did you become a camera operator and the second assistant camera for *Soldier*?

At the time, I had worked with first AC Bob Hall for a couple of years on various projects. This film came up when he interviewed DP David Tattersall. He got hired as A-camera first AC, and I was hired as the A camera second.

What kind of challenges did this movie provide to you, and which were the hardest, most enjoyable, funniest, and satisfying scenes or sequences to work on?

The biggest challenge was the extensive set built at Warner Bros Studios. Not only were we working on uneven surfaces all the time and high ledges, but the location was also filled with scrap aircraft parts that they brought in from God knows where. I was always brushing up against jagged aluminium from a fuselage. Nonetheless, the set was an incredible piece of construction. That is always the best part of my job—to see a massive crew construct a make-believe world that we get to film and sometimes blow up.

Filming the mini-gun fire was a rush. It was loud as hell and shook the stage, and it was like something grabbing your heart from the inside.

How long did it take to shoot the movie?

It was pretty close to a 70-day shooting schedule.

***Soldier* was set in the same universe as *Blade Runner* originally. Was there going to be a battle sequence at the shoulder of Orion and Tanhauser Gate?**

I was hoping there would be a flashback to these battles, but it is only referenced vaguely in the dialogue. The set pieces have links to *Blade Runner* since our production designer was the art director of the original film. The original drawings and moulds generated a foam copy of a "spinner" car.

What's your favourite memory or memories of working on the movie?

The big gravel pit in Irwindale where we destroyed everything.

What do you think of the movie personally?

It was a hard film, but fun to work on. I wish they would have expanded more on the *Blade Runner* theme.

Interview with Eric Dyson Film Loader

How do you get the assignment for *Soldier*?

So the lead first assistant focus puller was a guy named Bob Hall. I was on a television show before *Soldier* and, you know, we needed a couple of extra camera guys, so he came in. And I left that show early to start *Soldier*. And I think Bob has since retired, but, you know, this is how it happens a lot. You work with someone on one show, and they're looking for someone, and you kind of roll into these different circles. So I did *Soldier*, and then parts of one of Bob's mouse hunt movies. I worked with the camera crew. You know, different on different shows with different camera people quite a bit. On occasion, Alan Easton and I have worked together in that whole camera department over the years, although I never worked for the director of photography, David Tattersall, again. He was a great guy. Super nice guy.

How long did you work on the production?

It was probably six weeks, maybe eight weeks. Something like that. As you probably know, much of it was onstage at Warner Brothers [on] their most extensive soundstage, where that whole encampment was on the trash planet. And to see it in person was phenomenal. It just went up for all these zigzag trails that went back and forth from basically the ceiling down to a sub-level of the stage.

In terms of gear, it was gruelling. I don't think this is interesting to too many people as the loader. I was the film loader on the movie. My job was to make sure that whatever we shot was successfully taken out of the film magazines and sent to the lab. And, if you expose the film, it's terrible. But we were doing scenes way up in the top of the set. I had time to take the mag once they had to reload, and then run down and out the stage door before they would call rolling. And the scene was so long, and we could only do one take per mag, go to the truck, download it, put a fresh load in so that when they called cut I wouldn't have to run back up to the top layer of the set and hand them one mag and do it all over again.

The night exterior work was gruelling. The crawlers were shot in a rock quarry Northeast of downtown Los Angeles by Azusa. We'd have a three or four p.m. call and take all our stuff out of a hauling container. Everything had to get blown off and cleaned every day because so much dust and debris were flying around. And then we had rain some nights. And then, when it started getting light at about five o'clock in the morning, we would wrap and then come back the next day. A lot of the technology that they used at the time you either don't use these days or doesn't exist anymore; like when you have smoke, the things they used to be able to burn on set, like either rubber tires, or rubber cement, or the super toxic things are like a total no-go now.

It was shot on film, as well. It was pre-digital.

Yeah. There are shots where the crawlers come over the camera, right? And little what are called Imo's (small film cameras and steel housings). Those were custom made, and those are getting destroyed left and right either from an explosion or a crawler. It's mounted to a crawler, and that would go too close to another set-piece and rip that thing off. And whereas now it would either be a "GoPro" or a "Sony A Seven" or some other kind of disposable, basically digital technology. But back then, you had to think and plot this stuff out. And that's where David Tattersall, the cinematographer, was nice [and] soft-spoken. We didn't have walkie-talkies, and there was no texting back and forth. The irony between his soft-spoken demeanour and all these explosions and things was incredible.

Which sequences did you work on? Were you there for the whole shoot?

Yes. Some of it was farmed off to the second unit. I didn't have anything to do with it. The interior, a junk planet with all the community, was on stage. I was there for all that. All of the crawler stuff in Azusa, I was there for that. The training sequences and the stuff in the hangar in Santa Monica. Those scenes at the beginning with those rolling hills where all the troops were running and the little kids.

Were you there for the final fight sequence? You know, the fight between Todd and Caine?

That was my first experience of when an actor gets hurt. And it's the lead actor. And he says, "I'm going home." So this is where there's some big line-up sign falls, right? And Kurt Russell gets out of the way, and it just barely misses his foot. In one of the early takes, it hit the back of his leg in his Achilles. And we had to shut down for a couple of days because the lead guy got injured. It's like, did the special effects guy pull the wire too quick? Did Kurt Russell not have his foot out in time? Should we have used a stunt double? I was there for that sequence.

And all of these guns that they had [were] what you would put on an aircraft, like on a helicopter or mini-gun—these insanely loud guns. And I remember they would call action, and I would be probably 15 or 20 feet away, next to the camera, watching. The impact of these guns—you could feel the waves from the sound blast that the things would make. And then the shell casings that were all brass would rain like crazy for, I don't know, 20 or 30 seconds. They would call cut, and the guys would come and sweep up tons of these brass shell casings. And it seemed like they had an unending supply of ammunition. Talking about technology then versus now... Nowadays, most guns they shoot put the muzzle flash in post-production. But that was all the real deal. What you saw on camera was what we photographed with early digital Photoshop retouching. And I remember our still photographer showing me a picture that he shot of Kurt Russell next to one of these chains, and his muscles were all cut. Like, wow, he looks fantastic, right? And he goes, "That's Photoshop." Then he showed me the real one. And it was like, he's in great shape, but still, definitely not as much contouring cut to the muscles. But he says I'm not going to show that to Kurt. I'm only going to show him the retouched one. And now you have an app on your phone that adds six-pack abs. But not back then.

What were your favourite memories or memories of working on the film?

My favourite memories of the cast were all fantastic. And even though Gary Busey was a little weird, he was hard to figure out.... He'd had had this motorcycle accident a handful of years before, and you had heard all these stories about him. And he did not disappoint.

On Kurt Russell's birthday, Goldie Hawn came, and there was a cake with a stripper that jumped out of it. The stripper was an identical match to Goldie Hawn. She did it as a joke. And it was all very funny about the cake, and everybody had a good time. And another thing you couldn't get away with these days [is] when we did the stuff at the rock quarry in Azusa.

Every day at lunch, and lunch would be at midnight or one in the morning, I would go around with a big cart. And I would collect these big stones to use in my garden, which I still have. I would come home at four or five or six in the morning, leave my car. Then I would wake up at two or three in the afternoon, and my car was lowered to the ground because of all these rocks that I had collected. The on-set jokes between the other camera guys and me—it's like when you sit around for five or six hours waiting to do your first shot of the day. Inevitably, there's going to be plenty to laugh about. Allen Easton, the operator, was notorious for... We would have these headsets so he could communicate with the other people. And he would like randomly start singing some 50s style doo-wop song. Many of us would look at each other and shake our heads because we forgot our microphone was open.

What did you personally think of the movie when you saw it?

When I first saw it, I thought it was fantastic. You're just looking at all the scenes and remembering things. So the story's not sinking in. I've got to say, now that it's 25 years older or so, and you have a certain amount of more life experience, I don't feel like it holds up. Technically, it's a terrific-looking film. But there are a lot of things about it. Like, why is he dumped on a junk planet? And the point when the community decides, "Oh, we've got to have this guy back." It's a little bit contrived. And he's got this frown on his face because he's a badass killer. And the little kid also has a frown on his face, like, oh, well, they're gonna be a great duet, right?

I looked at the Rotten Tomatoes score on the thing, and it seems right. When it was over when I watched it, it was like, "Oh, this is almost the end of the movie." And the timing of it. The length was perfect, and you could always add these fight scenes and battle scenes. Those can go on forever. So, editorially, the editor did a great job. I love that sort of redemption moment when Kurt Russell's on the ship, and the door is going up, and these poor suckers are trying to get back into it. Then the ship leaves, and the bomb explodes.

It's structured well. It was supposed to be a bit like the Western *Shane*. So it's a throwback to simplistic Westerns and the 50s cavalry. Sure. Kurt Russell was inspired by John Wayne.

Yes. The things that made the Westerns successful. There was always something about the lead character you could relate to. And the level of their character arcs was not always huge, but there was some growth. And I think that was *Soldier's* downfall. Alright, I get it. He's not going to say too much. And at the end, he's still not saying too much. And this is a million-dollar actor, and he has the potential of bringing some of that to the screen. I don't know if it was a directing thing or what, but if you go to a movie to see Kurt Russell, I think you also want to hear Kurt Russell.

Interview with Actor Mark Bringleson (Rubrick)

How did you get cast?

The casting director (Mindy Merrin, who'd cast me earlier in Mick Jackson's film for Richard Zanuck, *Clean Slate*), sent my agent (Suzanne Jarrott, now deceased) the *Soldier* script and asked if I'd come in to talk with the director about playing Rubrick. I loved the screenplay, and originally, as I mentioned to you before, there was a sequence in the middle of the first draft that was about Rubrick wandering drunk among all the soldier guys in their bunks in the middle of the night, which I was crazy about but was cut before photography (the script was pretty long in its first draft). I met with director Paul Anderson and producer Jerry Weintraub at Jerry's office on the Warner Bros lot. We discussed the screenplay and the character, and then Paul asked if I'd read a couple of scenes, which I did. They were very friendly, very nice. I was struck at how young Paul seemed and how wise/Old Hollywood (a good thing, always) Jerry seemed. I thought the meeting went well.

I think my agent told me in a few weeks that the role went to someone else. So I forgot about it and went on to other projects. Then my agent called and said they were having a scheduling problem with the other actor, and the Rubrick role was now open. The director was requesting my reel to review my past work and that he'd liked me best of the other choices after their first guy.

My agent messengered my reel over to WB, and I think the next day they offered, and we made the deal. I was called in for a wardrobe fitting immediately, like within the hour. So we were off and running.

How did you prepare for the role, and what kind of discussions with Paul WS Anderson about it did you have?

I kept to my usual gym schedule (at that time)—4 days a week, lifting and every day in the gym additionally running two miles. I was also taking a fairly serious boxing class, and I continued that 2-3 days a week.

Soldier pre-shooting was the same for me as every film I did in regards to lines. Every day, I'd walk through each scene I was in, in order, by myself. I found out Michael Caine did this, and I stole it from him. I'd physically move around in some semblance of a set going through my dialogue. (I never did lines with a partner, only by myself.) I made lots of notes in the script (as I always did) in regards to Rubrick's history and past, and thought a lot about being isolated and away from loved ones. It seemed to me that Rubrick was very much alone in the film, although as I got to know some of my castmates (I didn't personally know anybody before the shoot) and we bonded (and played around) on the set in between scenes, some of that chemistry and affection I felt towards some of my fellow actors bled into the ensemble scenes when we shot, and I felt a bit less alone. Even so, that alienation and alone-ness was my foundation for the role.

I loved K.K. Dodds especially, who talked a lot about her boyfriend, who was in the punk band White Zombie, which interested me a lot. I equally loved Jason Isaacs, who was constantly hilarious in-between scenes and was always showing off some new tech gadget he'd recently purchased; Jason took movies of us, if I remember right. Also, Jason and and Paul Anderson were friends before the shoot, and their warm and supportive friendship was very welcome on that set. Kurt was usually elsewhere, he was alone and method, except one day when he brought a hot rod racing car to the set and showed it to everyone. Don't ask me about Gary.

Paul was very visually-oriented, and I loved standing behind or near him, watching him setting up shots. I learned a lot from him and how he shot and where he put the camera. (I was always shadowing film directors I worked with; I was very eager to learn from each by watching them work.) Paul was a great listener and full of compassion; I was crazy about him, but never said so out loud. I respected his responsibility to the film, which he was so great with. I felt he was very gifted and also a wonderful guy. His soon-to-be fiancée visited him on the set for several days, and the fun energy between them was pretty joyous to watch. One day, in-between takes, Paul talked (rather intensely) about his love for the cartoon show *Scooby-Doo*, which was amusing to me and Jason, if I remember, who also shared the same devotion.

Jerry Weintraub was on set many days, especially when Paul was shooting action stuff. He was a commanding presence, God knows, just sitting in his chair—I was aware of what a legend he was in the industry. He was very kind to me in his gruff way. Paul left me alone in creating Rubrick—it felt like he trusted me. I think we did most of the character talk in our original meeting in Jerry Weintraub's office, during casting. That's when I probably volunteered my thoughts on Rubrick being very much alone and alienated and trying throughout the film to connect with others but not succeeding, which Paul must've taken a liking to. His compassion and great focus during the shoot made all us actors feel great trust from him. He was generous that way. I'd look to him after a take; all he'd do was nod his affirmation.

What are your favourite memory or memories of working on the movie?

My Fave memory is the scene on the ship where I run to the others and exclaim, "People! I found people!" And then the scene after, as well, where K.K. and Jason and I got to work as an ensemble. Also, towards the end of the full shoot, we were covering an end sequence where Jason, K.K., and I were running on the planet terrain, and the three of us were on this huge, amazing soundstage on the Warner Bros lot, and they had these gigantic fans running, so it would appear real windy. We did several takes, and then Paul said they needed to turn off the fans just for sound. We did it without the fans going, and Paul came over to us and said, "What happened? You guys lost all your excitement. Let's do it again." And Jason and I pointed out that we were missing the wind effect. I said, "Paul, we're nothing without the fans." He got that sly British grin on his face and simply repeated my sentence, "You're *nothing* without the fans...," most sarcastically. Then he and I both laughed. But we turned the fans back on, and he liked the next take.

What do you think of the movie personally?

I'm very proud of the film. I think it's beautiful, moody, and somehow poetic. I only saw it once, the weekend it came out at the Chinese Theatre on Hollywood Blvd. So, it's been a long time.

DESIGNING
1234567890
SOLDIER
ABCDEFGHIJK
LMNOPQRSTU
VWXYZ

Interview with David L. Snyder Production Designer

How did you end up being a production designer?

I was educated in Buffalo, a Western New York city, at a secondary college prep school, that was a public school, meaning tuition-free. They had courses in architecture, engineering, and building construction. So, for three-and-a-half years, I studied architecture and, at the same time, I was working as a musician in a rhythm & blues band. At that point, I was making my education and my living as a student in the music business. Next, I got a job in an architect's office as a blueprint boy, and I don't think that job exists anymore, because we're in the digital domain. I felt like it was a place I belonged. But then along came an offer for me to join a band, which I did. And I went on the road for four years.

At the end of that period, I got a job in a major architectural firm in the Midwest, and I left the music business, because being on the road for four years was grueling. I decided that it would be a lot easier to stay in the music business as a record engineer, stay in one town and not have to travel, and at the same time, keep my day job as an architectural designer. So, after four years, I had an opportunity to relocate to California. I was working for an engineering firm in urban planning and civil engineering. It was a good experience. I didn't like the job that much, but I was still making a living and going to "play" every day because I've never actually worked a day in my life. At least it didn't seem like work to me. It was fun. I'd just go out to play, whether it was music, architecture, theatre, movies, or whatever thing that I was into.

At that time, the 1970s, the film industry in Los Angeles hadn't begun runaway production. I would say that eighty percent of all English language films were being made in Los Angeles, New York, Canada, the U.K. Commonwealth. So, the architectural-engineering firm assigned me to design a housing development called Rimrock Meadows, and it had a Cowboy-Western theme. I managed to get myself a pass to go on to the Paramount Studios lot in LA, where I visited the Western street. They wouldn't allow me to take any photographs, so I drew some pencil sketches.

They were shooting a Television series of worldwide fame entitled "Bonanza". I was on the set and I noticed a lot of people working as they were filming, and the crew would sit around drinking coffee and smoking cigarettes for like a half hour, and then, all of a sudden, when they finished a take, they'd all get up and do another setup, change the lighting, change the cast, whatever they did, then go back and sit down, smoke cigarettes, drink more coffee. I said, "This looks like a pretty good job." You work maybe less than half the time that you're there, the rest of it is waiting. And, of course, this is 35mm film, which is precarious and time consuming.

Then I met a guy, Jim Tompkins, who had a toy company and asked me if I would come to work designing toys. I thought, well, architecture and music and all the arts sort of crossover. I took a job with him. He had been an art director in network variety television shows like *The Julie Andrews Hour*. He decided he didn't want to do that anymore and he started this toy company. I worked with him and a staff of other terrific illustrators designing these toys. Jim went out to get a bank loan, and when the loan wasn't approved, he had to go back to work in television again. He called me up on a Friday afternoon, and he said, "I just got a job to be the art director at the 50th annual Academy Awards and I need an assistant art director, but you have to tell me right now, because if you don't, I'm going to hire somebody else." There I was working in my office as the in-house architect at an aerospace company, Teledyne Systems, and I said, "Okay, I'll do it." I left at noon that day and never went back.

The next day, a Saturday, we were at Paramount Studios, taking offices in the original 1920's dressing room building, which was in a shambles by the 1970s. The lot was empty except for Garry Marshall's television shows. It was literally a ghost town. We moved in, set up, and we began designing the 50th annual Academy Awards. It was quite exciting because we were also working at ABC Prospect Studios, which had originated as the 1913 Vitagraph Film Studios. Plus, the Dorothy Chandler pavilion for load-in and set-up based on production designer Tom H. John's designs.

Being the 50th Oscars, the entire show was sprinkled with legendary movie stars. Host Bob Hope, William Holden, Barbara Stanwick, Fred Astaire and Ginger Roger, and many more. So, it was amazing for me that within two months, to go from being the in-house architect in an aerospace firm to be working on the Academy Awards. More exciting that it was the year of *Star Wars* and *Annie Hall* nominations and wins. Directly after that, Jim said, "Okay, I've got another show from ABC. It's the Olivia Newton-John special with ABBA and Andy Gibb, and we're designing it." At the time, they all were the number one recording artists in the world. The show was recorded live with an orchestra in stereo. So, my first two shows were seen by millions of viewers. Five years later, in 1983, I was an Academy

Award nominee for *Blade Runner*. Very unusual to rise to that level within five years. That's where and how I started, and I've never stopped going. I was very lucky, and I loved my job.

How did you get the assignment for Soldier?

Warner Bros. was my home studio for a series of films. I did eight pictures there, including one for Columbia Pictures when Warner Bros. and Columbia shared the Burbank lot when it was officially the Burbank Studios. So, there I was at Warner Bros., and because I had done *Blade Runner* and *Demolition Man*, while waiting for the green light for *Soldier*, Warners hired me to design a concept for *Deep Blue Sea*, prior to Renny Harlin's involvement. As I was waiting, Jerry Weintraub and Susan Ekins, his producer, hired me to do *Soldier*. We began pre-production, and a lot of paintings and drawings and illustrations were created. Then, when Kurt Russell was hired, he said, "Okay, I'll do the film, but I want one year to prep for it." So, we shut down the Soldier A unit. Then, Jerry said, "David, I'm going to take over *Vegas Vacation* with Chevy Chase. Please come and do that with me and Susan and then we'll go back to *Soldier.*" It was great. I didn't have any down time in between Soldier A and Soldier B. We went to Las Vegas and had a good shoot. It was a fun movie. We met many great people on the cast and crew, then re-started Soldier 'A' at Warner Bros.

By that time, Paul W.S. Anderson and Jeremy Bolt were hired to direct and produce the film. So, Jerry and Susan Ekins sent me in to meet with Jeremy and Paul. There were other designers who were posting on social media stating that they had a meeting to do *Soldier* and they believed they were going to do it, but I was hired on the spot. I can't tell you why, but I was, and I got to spend a lot of money—more money on *Soldier* than on *Demolition Man* and, of course, on *Blade Runner* because it was many years earlier. So back to Warner Bros. I put a team together and the budget of building the sets was $10 million, and to decorate the sets was at least $2 million. The special mechanical effects, like creating the crawlers that had hydraulic systems that pushed the mock-up across the stage... The crawlers themselves were $500,000. A very expensive film at the time. The Art Department was massive and there were some people that I brought with me from *Demolition Man* and a lot of new people.

It was a very hectic job, because Warner Bros. had booked the picture for the next year before we even started, because that's the way studio distribution and exhibition used to be. Now with the introduction of streaming, it's different, as you know. Next, there was a weather prediction that there was going to be a huge storm that year. It's known as El Nino, a Southern California storm that occurs periodically. So, in a major meeting, I told the studio production execs Lorenzo di Bonaventura, Billy Gerber, Mark Scoon, Bill Young, and Bob Papazian, "Listen, if we build the village set in the quarry (where we would eventually film the bones of the spaceship Pandora), we could end up losing the village set in an El Nino flood." This meant they had to approve an additional $2 million to the construction budget. So, the village interior/exterior was approved to be constructed on famed WB stage 16.

In answer to your question regarding locations, Mike Fantasia was the location manager. We met on a Hollywood Pictures/Disney picture entitled *Burn, Hollywood, Burn: An Alan Smithee Film*, starring Eric Idle and others. Fred Caruso found him and introduced us. Mike came on at the last minute to replace someone who had dropped out. He saved the day. After that, I brought him onto *Soldier* and on *The One* starring Jet Li and Jason Statham. After that, I tried to get him on every film I designed. Once he started working for Steven Spielberg, it was hard to get him because he was a favourite of Steven's. Now he's with Martin Scorsese, as you probably know.

We had three eight hour a day shifts. We worked on that set 24 hours a day. The only days off were Thanksgiving and Christmas day to get it ready to film so they could release the film on the dates that they had scheduled. So, that's why that set alone was $1,200,000 to build in overtime. It was pretty spectacular. Next, we hired a set decorator, whom I hadn't worked with before. Her name is Kate Sullivan. She's lovely and she did such a terrific job. It was one of those shows where the construction department and set decorating had to work in tandem.

A lot of the components that were used in set decoration were things such as a full-size aircraft, a Japanese Shinkansen bullet train, full scale carved out of foam. The aircraft was a full size DC-3 airplane that we purchased from an aviation boneyard. We had to remove the wings to transport it to the studio. And then we had to load it into stage 16. Next, we loaded in tons of industrial "junk." We purchased helicopters and some of the objects that you see were found objects and some were manufactured from scratch. And, of course, people always asked me about the Syd Mead designed Spinner that we built from the original *Blade Runner* blueprints. It was just a goof, you know, for fun. An homage to Syd.

What exactly did you do as a production designer on the movie, and how close did you work with the set decorator Kate Sullivan and the prop department to get the right look for the movie?

Well, first of all, the way it worked out was extensive. The staff in the art department was responsible for certain disciplines, for example Tom

Valentine who was the visual effects art director. It was his job to coordinate between the visual effects department, which turned out to be ILM and many other VFX shops. At the end of the day, there were many people involved, and then there were people who were specifically coordinating with Joe Wood's construction department. As you know, there are always issues on the budget. The approved budget was $10 million, and Warner Bros. was very happy that we came in around $85,000 under budget. This was because Joseph E. Wood is very thrifty.

Then there were some in the art department who were building maquettes, a.k.a. clay models. The set went from one end of the stage to the other. It rose up 100 feet from below the deck. Then Joe Wood took the clay maquette and cut it into sections, and assigned a construction foreman to each section of the set. The tricky part of that is, each team is building a portion of the set out of plaster and wire and other required materials. At the end of the day, we hoped they would all fit together like a jigsaw puzzle. So that was very tricky. Paul Sonski, who was a supervising art director in charge of the drafting room and key art director of "Steelhenge," which we dubbed the skeletal remains of the Pandora ship. All of the designs of Simon Murton's illustrations, and the rest of the illustrators' conceptual works of art were painted in latex, oil, water color, and mixed-media. There wasn't much coordinating with transportation regarding picture vehicles with the exception of constructing the Crawlers out of earthmoving equipment. The tires on the vehicles were taller than an average-sized person.

We had stage 15, stage 16, and seven or eight sound stages at Warner Bros. We built the Soviet Union attack scene filmed in the ruins of the old Santa Fe Railroad shipping depot. At the time we filmed there, it was in desolate condition before it was turned into what it is today (the Southern California Institute of Architecture). Then there was the Barker Hanger at Santa Monica Airport.

There were no other vehicles on the Steelhenge set because everything dressed in the village was assumed to be components of the ruined ship Pandora. The set was constructed of steel that was fabricated in a factory and assembled on the site. It was four stories high and 500 Feet in length.

The day the cast and crew arrived, I was walking around the set, and suddenly, a golf cart from the transportation department comes flying in. Kurt Russell jumps off the vehicle to come over to thank me and said he'd never seen anything so spectacular. That was a great moment when someone from the cast admires and appreciates what the art department does.

At the end of the day on *Soldier*, we were lucky to have David Tattersall, who is the cameraman who shot a few of the *Star Wars* movies. He's great, and he lit that set with space-lights which were controlled by a lighting director via computer on a lighting board. So, the lighting cues for day and night and all the rest were all pre-set. That worked out great.

There's one spectacular shot in the film where the camera, on a cable-rig with an operator, goes from one end of the set up to the village door when Kurt Russell discovers the colony. As I recall, to get that shot, they began the move and rolled it back on the cable at high speed and then reversed the shot in post-production. This was a shot production designers dream of. I thank David for that ingenious shot of the entire set.

Were you inspired by anything particular in any of your designs to get the look you wanted for the film? And are there any sets that you'd like to discuss further?

One inspiring advantage was similar to working with Ridley Scott, then working with Paul Anderson, was their common interests in the output of the art department. Every detail.

Ridley and Paul spent equal time in the art department, and respected the art department. As you know, Paul is an artist in his own right, the same as Ridley. I enjoy working like that. Then, there are other films, working with people like say, Carl Reiner. When I worked with Carl and Linda De Scenna, the set decorator of *Blade Runner*, we were free to do whatever we wanted. Carl's thing was writing and performance. I always say that my inspiration is the script. My job is to take those words and turn them into pictures. That's my model. So, if you look at *Soldier*, and then look at *Super Mario Bros.*, there isn't much in common visually except just filling the frame, you know, overloading the frame. And then some films that are minimalist, like my Jet Li film, *The One*.

I try to inspire the staff to inspire me. The first sketch I did on *Soldier* was when it was going to be in the quarry. It's a Pentel sketch I did, and I said, "Okay, here's the village, here's Jimmy The Pig's place, this and that." It's sort of a conceptual drawing; a layout of where things go. And sometimes I'll take a blank piece of paper and draw circles and say, "Okay, this goes here, that goes there." Because of my training in architecture and urban planning, I think about the movement more than the aesthetics. The "art" comes later. Where the camera's going to be, where the crew is going to be, what the set-ups are, and where the sun will be for natural daylight is primary. Then I lay everything out in plan as an architect or an engineer would do to show that it's able to function. Because if it doesn't function, all the beauty illustrated in the conceptual drawings won't matter. Then, of course, I have to consult with my construction coordinator and set decorator, because you have a responsibility to spend only the money the studio or production budgets for the sets.

On *Demolition Man*, I had a very tough time with the city not wanting us to shoot at the brand-new Los Angeles Convention Center. I had to put on a jacket and tie and go to a meeting with the location manager and the administration. The way we convinced them that we needed to be filming the new convention center as San Angeles Police Headquarters was, in effect, our apology for making Los Angeles appear in ruin in *Blade Runner*. So, there's a lot of politics involved in what I do.

It takes many skills to be a production designer, as opposed to an art director. And a lot of it has to do with politics; a lot has to do with convincing people and using the tools to convince them, whether it's a drawing, or a model, or just the right pitch that a director responds to.

Interview with Mike Fantasia Location Manager

How did you end up being the location manager on *Soldier*?

I worked with David Snyder before *Soldier* on a movie called an [*Burn Hollywood Burn:*] *An Alan Smithee Film*. It was the last movie directed by Arthur Hiller, one of the last of the old-time Hollywood directors. David and I are both from upstate New York and bonded right off the bat. After we worked on the Smithee film, David called me and told me his next film won't have a lot of locations, but it would be a difficult film with a lot of pyro and logistics. So I went in, met with the production manager and the producers, and got the job. So, David Snyder brought me on.

How did you prepare for the project, and what kind of challenges did the movie provide you? Were there any problems with permit locations and production material?

There were a lot of problems on the film. The quarry where we built the otherworldly landscape is in the northeast part of Los Angeles County, in Irwindale and Azusa. It's an 80- or 100-foot-deep quarry. We went in with 'dozers and graded it so there was a bit of a slope so that water would run off when it rained

We never expected it to be an El Nino year in Los Angeles. We got a shitload of rain, weeks and weeks of rain. And we didn't have enough slope. And when you're 80 feet below the surface, that's where all the water goes. We dug a huge sump hole and water drained into that. We set up a pump, and we ran a couple hundred feet of fire hose to a place where the water would be deposited. My assistant, Michael Aycock, started at the far end, and he ran hose to the pump. And when he got to the pump, he discovered he laid the hose the wrong way—the male end to the male. And it was raining like a mother. He had to reverse all of that, and we eventually got the pit pumped out, but it was a wet, messy, awful situation. By the time we filmed, it had cleared up enough that we didn't have problems, but that was a challenging location.

Also, we had massive gunfire in the scenes we filmed there. The studio said we had to do some sound tests, so we brought in a sound engineer. We thought that fog would muffle the sound, but instead, the fog reflected the sound, so instead of the sound travelling a few hundred feet, it travelled well over a mile into the adjacent neighbourhoods. So, we notified all the neighbours [and] we put some people in hotels, but it was a huge ordeal dealing with the sound issues.

At Big Sky Ranch, where we shot a couple of locations, once again, [there was] a lot of rain. We got all the trucks and equipment in, we shot our scenes, and as we turned around to get the trucks out at the end of the day, one truck got stuck. Another truck tried to go around him. Of course, you can't go off-road into a field. So, we had five or six semis stuck up to the hubs. The whole crew was backed up; the actors were backed up, and people had to get out of their cars and walk around this mess, getting wet and muddy, to get into vans that shuttled them to the base camp. And it took a couple of days afterward to get all those trucks pulled out of there. It was just it was a nightmare.

How was the experience working with the cast and crew there?

David Tattersall, the DP, is just a great guy. Nice fella. And his whole team was excellent. David always has a great art department. His set decorator, his art directors, his construction crew were fantastic. And you're always laughing with David. He's such a funny guy. One night, we were shooting at Warner Bros. We had an interior hospital scene, and we used an office at Warner Bros. So, we're sitting there at probably three o'clock in the morning. You know, you're punch drunk; you're exhausted. We're sitting in a golf cart. David told me a story from his early Hollywood days. It was one of the most hysterical stories I've ever heard. We were laughing uncontrollably. I almost peed my pants. It was it was just hysterical.

How was the hangar set, and where was it located?

We shot that at the Barker Hangar at the Santa Monica Airport. It's a World War II Quonset hut, a cool old hangar. One of the few left. Most of them have been torn down and replaced with more modern hangars. It's not used for aviation anymore. It was hard juggling our dates to fit their schedule, because they had so many bookings. They had these substantial fashion shows, car shows, and other things like that.

We had to paint the floor with a special paint that can withstand heavy use, because when an airplane turns, it'll tear the paint. It probably cost $100 a gallon at the time. I can't imagine what it costs now. We painted the floor, and then we painted a seal in the middle of the floor. I had only managed a couple films at the time, but I'd already learned that the paint department usually was the department that was an enormous pain in the ass when they age buildings. "Oh, it'll come off." *It never comes off!* Anyway, there was a huge problem when they went to take the seal off. The seal also took the paint off underneath. You don't just repaint part of it. You must repaint it all. So, it was a massive pain in the ass and a considerable cost to repaint that floor because of the seal. But that was a great location. And the best part about it [was that] it was a quarter of a mile from my house. So, I could virtually walk to work.

Were there any scenes or sets that weren't used in the film?

I don't think so. We had around 10 locations. We didn't have a lot of locations. We had the pit, the hangar, Big Sky Ranch, and an old hipping warehouse that now houses SciArc in downtown LA. Trains would come in on one side and cargo would be offloaded from the trains into trucks on the other side. We did that scene where they had a shootout and explosions in that surreal location. So, in the old days, you would drive by it, and there would be these open bays, and the garage doors were all torn off. You go by, and you'd look right through the building. And today, there are big condos in the parking lot. That was our base camp. And if you drive by, you see students and professors in their offices and classrooms. In those days, downtown L.A. was a ghost town. You could shoot all night; there was nobody living there. Now, it's thriving again, and all those great locations that we used to have are virtually all gone. It's challenging to shoot down there.

What did you think of the movie personally when you first saw it?

I couldn't get into Kurt's character. I didn't connect with it. I thought the sets were fantastic and that Junk Planet set that David built on the stage was incredible. You'd never build that set today. You'd build part of it and CG the rest. Joe Wood, the construction coordinator, and Matt Sanders, the welder, both had incredible, incredible talent; tremendous talent. And because the weather was so bad that winter, everywhere we went, people pulled together when the shit was hitting the fan, when trucks were getting stuck and sets were flooded. Everybody did what they had to do to make things work.

The location in Azusa is diagonally across L.A. County from where I lived in Mar Vista. I would have to fight rush hour traffic coming home at sunrise. It got to the point where I was sitting in traffic for two hours, falling asleep in my car, exhausted. So there were many nights when we were filming the quarry that I just stayed in a hotel in Irwindale. The nights were long. I had one assistant who was working on prepping other sets. I was on set at night. And during the day, you've got to do permits, get permissions, get signatures, do all the paperwork, and work 18 to 20 hours a day. I was so new at being a location manager. I would never do that today. I would have two or three more assistants, and I'd be doing the day shift, and they'd be doing the night shift. But you know, when the shit's hitting the fan, and it's raining, and sets are flooding, you've got to be there.

All in all, it was a great experience. First, working with David Snyder is always a trip. It's always fun. Always a laugh. You're always laughing. So that makes it a lot easier. It was a fun experience. I learned a lot. I increased my knowledge immensely, quantum leaps from where I was before that because of a lot of the problems we had. And you learn a lot when you work with somebody like David. He's a great designer, and he's a great guy. I wasn't young, I had a career before I got into the film business, but I was new, so he helped me out a lot.

Interview with Kim Bailey Assistant Art Director and Technology Designer

How did you end up working in the film industry?

Easy. It was blackmail, either that or work for the government... just kidding. I took a summer job in 1976. One thing led to another, and for some unknown reason, the veterans of the business let me hang around them and learn. It was Pete Gerard on *Galactica* that gave me my first steps, and then Danny Lee on the Disney lot for *The Black Hole* that cemented me in the business. From there, it was a long string of shows, non-union education, and picking up any bit of skill and information I could get.

How did you get the assignment to be the technology designer for *Soldier*?

Tom Valentine knew me from Apogee and other shows like *Deep Impact* and the like. He knew by that date and time I had owned and operated Starlight Effects, where we had done a ton of work, including building the Borg

Ship for *Star Trek: The Next Generation*. Tom had me meet David Snyder, who looked at my skill set, the number of pictures I had supervised, and my electronics background, and literally gave me a blank check to design, build, and supervise multiple elements for the show.

What exactly did you do as the assistant art director and technology designer on the movie, and how close did you work with the production designer, David L Snyder, and the art department to get the right look for the movie?

Tom was buried with all manner of agenda items [and] Clay Penny had his hands full with all the major FX that were happening, so David let me hire my own 44 effects crew (people I had hired from other shows where Tom and I worked together), and both Tom and David set me to work designing technology, blinky lights, elements for set dressing, and the entire control and command console for the daddy cockpit. It was the first time I was set forth as a true assistant art director role but held the title of technology designer.

Many times David would just say, "Go do it. I trust you, and you know what you are doing." When David saw the results of what was being created, much to the pleasure of the director, he then turned me to the crawlers where I was tasked to completely build the interior look and science. Granted, *Soldier* was a number of decades ago, and I was so busy on that show moving from art department to 44 Effects (held two union cards, one for local 44 and one for local 800), that may of the elements that I personally did blend into the set as if they were meant to be there. Tom Valentine gets the big nod on the crawlers, and I was really thankful when Tom asked me to assist to get it all done for camera.

Were you inspired by something particular in any of your technology designs to get the look you wanted for the movie, and are there any sets or scenes you'd like to discuss further?

That is a very difficult question, and the answer is going to be even more bizarre. I suffer from the Hitchcock syndrome for professional filmmakers. Years after I had entered the business and had gotten my knuckles scraped and literally bled on a few shows, I met the Richard Fleischer, who at the time I had no idea of who he was or what he had accomplished. Richard was just one of those veterans I would ask questions of to learn the wisdom from the golden age of film. One day when speaking about film history (and believe you me, if you are a professional filmmaker, you had better know your film history), he told me that Alfred Hitchcock suffered from a condition that he could see a movie in his head with all the music, sounds, lighting, sets, camera angles, actors, blocking, and performances as if the movie played in his mind well before any frame of film was exposed. Years later, I became close friends with Richard Bennett, who worked with Doug Trumble on *Close Encounters*, who told me the very same story.... So it had to be true. I confided in Richard (both of them) that the same thing happens to me when someone tells me a story or asks me to collaborate on a project. It is this weird and almost spooky thing where I know what to do without ever having a day of education or exposure to a setting. Yes, I have had moments where I'm shaking in my boots and am seriously nervous from time to time of the "can I really do this?," but then, all of a sudden, the light opens up and it becomes all too clear to me. So with *Soldier*, I was captivated by the storyboard and Tom Valentine's illustrations. It gave me a storytelling setting to ground my basis of science fiction and science fact. The visuals just came to me for that show, and at each turn, Tom and David just shook their heads happily and said, "Keep going."

As for this and other shows and inspiration, in the beginning I was instructed by Pete Gerard when I started in the business to read everything you can, subscribe to every free technical and periodicals publications you can, attend every free seminar on every kind of manufacturing there is from mould making to you name it." So I did, and by the time I was 25 I was receiving over 100 publications every month on every subject I could get. I know now, it was that decade of absorbing everything, meeting and becoming friends with scientists at places like JPL, Lawrence Livermore Labs, MIT, and CalTech that seated my theoretical science. On the creative side, I had made deep friendships with people behind the scenes who made Hollywood glamorous, and I will never be able to thank them fully for the deep appreciation of those who came before me.

Advanced avionics and technology design like that of the shuttle cockpit and other tech for *Deep Impact*, or the science for *Space Above and Beyond* and *Mission to Mars* was the result of that gift. As for one of the most influential and impactful moments, it had to be *Stargate* for Dean Devlin. I was brought on as a consultant to solve challenges that would arise, and for the most part, I knew personally almost every department head. There is far too much to tell about that amazing project, but as for crossing the creative style line from technology to Egyptology, *Stargate* was a real stretch of my creative skills and solving challenges for the show.

Can you give us an example or examples of how you used the symbolic aspects to a character in a set or scene in the movie?

Robert Duvall said it best. I think that when a set is done right, it is like a costume they put on, and setting for an actor. Every project I have done has been vastly different from the next. *Stargate* had the glyphs and carvings, the first CNC 3D set pieces for a film, and the ring transporter I designed, which they still use for TV. *Mission Impossible* had all the toys, like the retina scanner. *Strange Days* had the trodes and playback devices. *Alien Resurrection* had the labs, halls, and cockpits. *The One* had our special alphabet created for it along with a bunch of science for the tunneler and the multiverse. *Space Above and Beyond* had multiple elements from the flight deck to the SA-43 cockpits all through the season. *Mission to Mars* was a very high-end living/breathing set for both the Recovery Spacecraft and Mission Control. Many of the elements I have designed as story points that were pure science fiction have since become science fact.

Which scenes or sets were the most challenging or fun to do, and what are you personally most proud about regarding your own work on the film?

Mission to Mars, by far, has to be hands down the most challenging feature film I have ever had the honour of working on. I ran four departments for that production, including all the technology design for the picture. It is where I became good friends with the legendary astronaut Story Musgrave, the man who developed and ran the program to save the Hubble telescope. *Mission to Mars* started on the Disney lot for me in California, but I ended up spending almost a year in Vancouver, Canada working on the show, many times flying back and forth to Los Angeles to handle logistics. There are so many elements on *Mission to Mars* that came together, but I have to say it was the entire team of people who I had the honour to work with that helped make that magic happen.

I can say I designed the entire cockpit for the recovery vehicle along with story points effects that Brian De Palma wanted. In one very scary meeting, Brian had assembled the entire film's leadership to discuss the pivot point of the movie, saying we need to find a way to get them from the ship to the planet. Brian was stumped as to what the actors would say and what actions would be taken, and in a moment of panic for myself, Brian De Palma turned to me and said, "You're the tech genius, what would they say and do?" I rattled off a few things off the top of my head with some embellishment to the original script. It stopped Brian in his tracks, and he said, "That's great! write it...!" I immediately turned to Sam Mercer, the executive producer, and asked, "Can I do that?" To which he replied, "He said to do it, so yeah." I wrote 20 pages of dialogue for the script of *Mission to Mars*, and Brian De Palma shot every word of it as if he had come up with it himself. I did not know to be frightened out of my mind or buy a lotto ticket once I had completed the task. All I do know is that Brian and I became friends after that where if there was a science question on the show or something the actors needed to do that looked right, I was told to "direct the actors and help them get this right." *Wow!* Even today, writing this, brings me back to a pinnacle moment of my career.

What's your favourite memory or memories of working on *Soldier*?

I have so many favourite films and TV shows that I have worked on. It goes like this, each time we come together to work on a project, no matter how big or small, it can and many times does, become a family. You meet so many new people and get to know them in a creative environment where we inspire each other to reach beyond what we ourselves think is possible. Sure, there are the moments of drama, politics, and those who feel the business owes them something, but the true artists look at their career as an honour to be able to participate. We cherish every single moment we have because for most of us, we know beyond any reasonable doubt, our time here on earth is limited and our time working in film is even shorter.

With *Soldier*, my best memories are working side by side with my dear friend Tom and getting to know David Snyder of *Blade Runner*, who became one of my best friends. Yet, it is the many crews I had the honour to work with, like Clay Penny's team, getting to know and work with Kate Sullivan, the set dec, and then my own small effects crew of 4 lead by Don Krause, and everyone in between that I treasure the most. *Soldier* was more than a simple movie for me; it was a time that allowed a freedom of design and trust I had not yet been given. To say thank you seems pale by comparison to the gratitude I feel for the work done.

What do you think of the movie personally?

It could be so much more. It had all the right pieces to make a splash. It did not get the chance to be the film it should be. I still like the film for its simplicity and epic scale of design by David. It also holds a special place since I had one more chance to say hello to Gary and Kurt, since we had crossed paths on previous films together.

Interview with Jon Danniells Art Department

How did you end up working in the art department?

I was working for a moving company called Starving Students, and a high school friend's mom asked if I do sort of the same thing for a movie for a few days until their regular guy could get there. I did a good enough job that they kept me on for the entire production.

How did you get the assignment to be the lead man for *Soldier*?

I honestly don't remember. I knew the decorator socially, and when she got the job she asked me to be her lead.

Were you inspired by something particular in any of your designs to get the look you wanted for the movie, and are there any sets or scenes you'd like to discuss further?

As the lead, my job is to coordinate and help realize the vision of the set decorator and the designer. That said, I felt CD's were going to be going the way of the 8-track, so I made the equivalent of a beaded-curtain out of them, as well as a few chandeliers. The production designer had worked on *Blade Runner*, so it was a great honour to work with him. I had worked with Ridley Scott on the first commercial I ever was a lead on, and then years later on *GI Jane*.

Which scenes or sets were the most challenging or fun to do, and what are you personally most proud about regarding your own work on the movie?

Creating the massive mountains of garbage that needed to stand up to 70 mph winds (that never really came to pass, at the most some large ritter fans, but I was told to be prepared for it). We brought in several semi-trucks full of airplane salvage from a great source out in the middle of Mojave, El Mirage, California called The Aviation Warehouse.

What's your favourite memory or memories of working on the movie?

Rappelling from the perms onto the wings of Stealth bomber that was buried in the mountain of garbage.

What do you think of the movie personally?

Honestly, it's not my cup of tea. But we had a lot of fun on the project, and I made some lifelong friends.

Interview with Peter Montagna Makeup Artist

How did you end up working in makeup effects?

I started in the early 80s when I started working in the business. I was doing it as a hobby. I was interested in it and interested in commercial art, so I thought I might be an artist. It's a long story how I got into it, but I lived in New York at the time. I grew up in New York. The three major networks, CBS, NBC, and ABC, had network apprenticeships where you serve 18 months as an apprentice to get hired. Then, after 18 months, you're eligible to take your union test and become a journeyman. I applied for the ABC, and I didn't get it. Still, as luck would have it, I did get the NBC apprenticeship, so I worked on all the NBC TV shows. So I started in television.

I didn't start in film.

I met Steve Laporte, the key makeup artist on *Soldier*. Steve is from California, and he was in town working on a music video for the rock group The Cars. The video had all these wacky makeups, synthetic aliens, and things like this kind of a space thing, so he needed someone to help him out. He got my name from Dick Smith, who I had worked alongside. One of the reasons I got the apprenticeship was because of a recommendation from Dick, because I was corresponding with him when I was starting. He liked my work, which gave me a push to get the apprenticeship.

But Steve needed someone to help him out, and we worked out of his hotel room getting all these masks and things ready. Steve is a great guy. We had a mutual love for makeup, and he is a terrific guy to work alongside. I've known him my whole career. When I finally made a move out to L.A., I worked with Steve on a lot of projects. I hired him, he hired me, and Steve was the department head, an exceptional makeup designer on *Soldier*. Dennis Lidiard was Kurt Russell's personal. Sometimes that happens in your career. You will hook up with someone that likes you, and you become like a star request. So Dennis was Kurt's guide, and Dennis, his father, was a makeup artist who had a long working relationship with Robert Redford. Dennis knew Steve, and then I wound up working with Dennis. I hired Dennis, and he hired me, so we were always in a working relationship. That's how the three of us got the job on *Soldier*. Dennis got the project and needed someone to do these special makeups, so I was the second, and Steve was the department head. That's how I got the job for *Soldier*.

The scale and production were unbelievable for *Soldier*.

You could tell when they're spending money. The sets were fantastic. We shot that at Warner Bros. at stage 16, which is the enormous soundstage in North America. They shot *Goonies* there, *Jurassic Park*, and the last *Indiana Jones* was shot there. There's like a water tank below the soundstage to retract the sound stage, and then they can build a water tank, so the pirate ship sequence on *Goonies* was shot there. They built the Mayan temple for *Indiana Jones*. I was working on the lot. In doing another show, and for nine months, I watched them build that Mayan temple. It was spectacular, so that's where they shot the derelict planet for *Soldier*, and it was quite a set. They had a lot of full-size props. They had a full-size train, all kinds of wild stuff, if you could believe it. They even replicated one of the spinners cars from *Blade Runner*. It was amazing. When I saw the spinner car, it was like half-buried on a set, but I looked at it and said, "That looks familiar." I walked over to it, and I said, "This is the spinner car from *Blade Runner*." I said, "Holy smoke, they're using props from the older movies." But it was quite a set. It was terrific. And then, of course, there was the lower level where the colonists lived. It was spectacular. But that's the enormous soundstage in North America, so I could see why they used that for the production.

I think the production was such an epic undertaking for its time. It was filmed in Azuza, right?

Yes, it was—the good old gravel pit. I will tell you a funny story. They had these vehicles called crawlers, and to give them more sense of scale, they had men on top of the crawlers. They were driving on top of them or in the vehicle. To make the vehicles look more extensive, they hired little people, dressed them in costume, and put them on the vehicles so the crawlers would look more expansive. It was a little trick that they did, and that's why if you watched the movie, you might pick up on it.

On the tattoos of the soldiers:

If I remember correctly, we decided where we would put a tattoo. The forehead was kind of out of the question because that would look kind of goofy. And we opted to put it on the side of the face, or I think at one point, we thought maybe the neck was even a possibility. But that was always getting braided by a collar, so the most likely spot was the cheek. It also looks badass to have something on your cheek like that.

We had to do makeup on Brenda Wehle, who plays Hawkins. She's kind of like the spokesperson for the colonists. And at one point, she gets incinerated. So, we had to do something basically out of the kit. And out of the kit makeup is something that you don't have much time to prep for. So you use basic materials. And on the day, you create a makeup that's basically out of a kit. Usually, if it's a unique makeup, you have the option of having a live cast of the actor, and you can sculpt and make moulds and make them and make something it's moulded. It's custom-fit to the actor, and you have that luxury. We didn't have that luxury. But they wanted to show half of her face being burned away. Brenda had very curly red hair. And we had to figure out a way to hide all her hair. Usually, you'd put a ball cap on someone, and you'd have a wig that represented her that looked like her own hair, and you'd have part of it removed, but we didn't have the time to make a wig.

So, Steve and I brainstormed and came up with a way of taking our hair, flattening it against her skin, and then putting the pieces over that. So that eliminated her hair. We used gelatin sheets that looked like burnt skin. And we put that on, then we painted it, and she had a contact lens in her eye, and it looked superb.

It was gruesome-looking when we finished it. But that's one of the challenges we had to, you know, sometimes you have. You don't have prep time, and you must come up with ways of making things work. Sometimes, they'll shoot it and realize it's a little too gruesome. So, they'll cut it out; they won't quite feature it. Now, there are a lot of decisions that get made in cases like that. Or, sometimes, the opposite happens. Sometimes you'll do something, and they love it. And they'll tell you we're not really going to see it, and then they like it so much that they feature it. I've had that happen, too, so you never know. You weren't quite prepared for it to be seen. But they liked it so much that they featured it.

Memories of Kurt Russell:

He's a good sport and a wonderful guy to work with. He was a child actor. He started working at Disney, and he became excellent friends with Walt. Walt was very fond of him. Kurt told us many stories about growing up on the lot. He is an earnest and outstanding actor, but he doesn't take himself too seriously. Kurt takes the work very seriously, but you can kid around with him. He's very good-natured and a lot of fun. We used to have a lot of fun with him in the trailer. He was great to work with.

I understand, if I remember, he prepared for the movie with almost a year of training because he was in fantastic condition. If I recall, Kurt wound up fracturing his foot when part of the set fell on his foot. It was quite a physical undertaking. It was a very physical movie as well. At the end of the film with Jason Scott Lee, the fight was intense. Dick Zeiker was the stunt coordinator on that.

What were some of the challenges of doing the makeup?

One of them was shooting that end fight sequence in the rain. And Jason Scott Lee had appliances on him. He had a scar, and Steven Laporte designed and created it. Steve and I were trying to figure it out. It was made of gelatin; typically they're rubber appliances, but we didn't like how rubber looked, so we went with gelatin. Gelatin was being used because it's very translucent, and it's easier to make it look like skin and flesh than rubber because it has acceptable quality. We thought it would be perfect to use on Jason. It just melts when it gets wet, so we had to figure out how to seal it. So we devised a way to waterproof it, which was one of the challenges in that sequence. Also, I had to build a prop arm of Jason Scott Lee when Kurt breaks it and hyperextends it at one point in the fight.

We needed a fake arm of Jason, so we utilized the Warner Bros. lab, which is no longer there. A fellow named Bob Noren, whose family was in makeup going back to the 30s, let us use the lab. We took an impression of Jason's arm so it would match perfectly. Then I fabricated a fake arm that looked like his, and we rigged it so his arm was behind his back. Then we shot it at such an angle it looked like his arm. I oversaw building it. That worked well. It was just one of those things we had to do during production. Things come up all the time.

That sequence is very effective.

It was very intense. I don't know how long it took to shoot that, but it was a big undertaking. I also remember when we did the character of Mace, Sean Pertwee was the actor. He gets his leg blown off. That was just a foam fabrication we did in the trailer that was just improvised and painted to look like a stump, which is all we needed, really. Most of the wardrobe covered it, and we had some tubes running under the dirt, and we just pumped some blood, and it was effective.

What was your reaction to *Soldier* when seeing it?

I thought it was a good movie. I enjoyed it. When you watch a movie that you worked on, it's hard to watch it objectively because you're always thinking about what was happening when they were shooting that film.

I remember this, and I remember that you kind of know how the magic trick was done, so it takes a little bit of the freshness out of it. If I haven't seen a movie that I worked on for a long time, I can appreciate it as a movie. But it's hard to watch a film that you worked on because you're so familiar with it. It takes the uniqueness out of the film. You have a different perspective when watching the movie; you can appreciate it for what it is, but the people who worked on it have an insight into it that the average person doesn't.

A good movie is a good movie. I can still enjoy it. I thought *Soldier* was a good movie, and Kurt was good.

Interview with Steve LaPorte Key Makeup Artist

How did you get the assignment for *Soldier*?

I worked with Jerry Weintraub on three films. I can't say enough good things about Jerry. He was a great guy. He was a very hands-on producer, and you know, if I had issues with actors a couple of times, he stepped in. He was a guy in my corner, and I always appreciated that. I was his guy. I did *The Next Karate Kid*, and then I did *The Speialist* with Jerry. That's where I exhibited a lot of my effects stuff on the specialist, some gags, and fake heads. Then as we got into working on other things, he offered me *Vegas Vacation.* Peter Montagna was living in Vegas at the time. He was on another project, so I tried to pass the ball. You know, you always try to give the ball to other people that I work with, and that didn't work. So it's a little break from working with Jerry because he is a great guy to work with.

Then he called me for *Soldier.* That was the biggest budget makeup one that I ever did with Jerry. I came from having a studio to getting rid of a studio to building a small one behind my home, so I was doing small scale stuff. And then when *Soldier* came along, I was working on the patio and in my shop. Dennis Liddiard, who was Kurt's personal, came in, and knowing that we had two main characters that we had a lot of stuff on them, it worked out great because he and I would double team Kurt to get him out of the chair quickly. Because Kurt had a boxer's eye and a bunch of scars and stuff, and the tattoo thing was a deal we did. But basically, once I spent my half hour with Kurt, Dennis would finish him up and carry on with him all day and he and I could switch off watching him. So if he needed a break, I could do that, and Peter was my right hand man as far as some of the other peripheral characters. Sometimes a real sweet makeup camp comes up, and Peter would jump on it, and I'd help him out. And you'd cover it all day, and then Jason Scott Lee probably had the most extensive makeup all the time because he always had a scar, and he always had a contact lens. When they decided to do the ripped out eye gag, I said, "This guy's got to do fighting, and because he's using martial arts in his acting portion he needed his depth perception, so let's put a contact lens out and give him a really cool subtle surgical repair of his eye." That's when we went to the low profile kind of scarring.

That scarring was later on in the picture.

Yes, and I didn't want to go with the classic keloid scars, because Kurt had this big keloid scar. So, I went with something puckered and pinched like they had lasered it together. I wanted it to look like a more futuristic type of repair, but also mash in the field repair. The way they presented this whole film was all like an industrial society. I went through several tests. I still have the moulds for Jason. I use the pieces for stock pieces.

When Kurt and Jason fight on the chains, how did you do the eye gouge gag?

We did it in reverse. We did the heavy makeup first, so Jason was in the chair, and we did the end of it first. Then I could clean them up and go back and shoot all the leading up stuff to it. We had to climb the ropes and get him ready that way; production didn't have to wait for me to go and put the makeup on for them to do that one little bit. There was a movie I saw a long time ago called *Zombi*. It's an Italian horror film where a woman is on the side of a door, and a fist breaks through the door, and all these splinters come out. It grabs her by the hair, and it pulls her slow-motion cut back and forth of her eye being pulled towards this splinter, and it sticks in her eye and breaks off and peels. It rips the skin, so that was kind of in the back of my head, thinking for *Soldier*, well, if he thumbs the eye and then pulls, that's what would happen. We had to cut away some time later with the eyepiece, which was very subtle. Still, I made everything out of gelatin so I could do multiple tests and not wait on lab time, and gelatin at the time was making a comeback because it was so natural, translucent, fast to put on, and not that durable.

They changed the scene at the end to the rain after the makeup was all done, and we hadn't started using silicone at that time. So, I put so many coats of plastic sealer on his face that he looked shiny, but it worked fine because he was all wet and polished from the water. We shot that fight scene for a week, and one time I had to change it out because if gelatin gets wet, it swells up and just pops loose and comes off the skin. Fortunately, I lived close by, so if I had to run home to get something from the lab or make stuff at night, I could. But basically, I sculpted like three versions of scars and chose the one that they liked best, and then I would make them in the trailer. I could microwave the gelatin, put it in the moulds, flame it together, go to set, come back and make another one. Kurt had the same thing. He had a gelatin eyepiece, and we only had to change his once.

I've worked on *Terminator 2: Judgement Day,* and coming off and knowing all the underlying look of those films. When I read this, Kurt's regime, and the group of soldiers he was trained in were old school. And then the Caine character, [who] were these genetically produced soldiers. Soldiers must communicate in the field. Now they wear tiny earpieces. It's gotten more modern. It used to be walkie-talkies. But I wanted to do a prosthetic on all the Caine line of soldiers, like a built-in device under the skin.

So, every character would have required a prosthetic. And it just was going to be too elaborate. It was subtle, and the one character would have been great. But when you have a whole line of soldiers that all look alike... and originally Jason showed up to my shop because I had to do a cast on him. And here on the first day of rehearsals, he showed up and shaved his head. Jerry flips and says, "I hired an actor with hair. How come he shaved his head?" So, then all the soldiers in his group, we had to shave everyone's head because we're going to put bald caps on anybody.

Kurt had that great flattop look, and then the tattooing turned out to be relatively simple, but it was the names they wanted. They wanted everyone's name and blood type. So, ideally, if they got hurt in the field, they could just identify them because the dog tags were old school. So, they wanted everyone's face tattooed.

At the beginning of the film, you see his record. And it has all the references, kind of Easter eggs, of all the roles he had.

We made two versions of tattoos. We had a full one. It went all the way up to the shoulder for when his shirt was off. But when he wore the shirt, we cheated and made a little short one so we could tuck it up under. We'll just keep it there to save time because it was always going to rub off. The only trick was the polo shirt off in the shot, and we had to make sure we had the whole run. But then that had to be there for a limited amount of time because the tattoos would just rub off. Sweat and perspiration, and the shirts were so tight. So, we just cheated a little bit. And Kurt was the only one which saw many of those tattoos on some of his other guys. We showed a few of them, but we never saw any of them when they Caine group because those were new soldiers.

With the makeup of the colonists and the military guys, did you want a contrast, like making the soldiers look gritty and the colonists look cleaner?

Because they're on a planet with a lot of wind stuff, we chose to put an airbrush red on everybody, just to red everybody up. And we had to make it an assembly line. We made it simple. You know, they didn't want anyone to look made up. So, it was, you know, catch as catch can. You run people through, and I've done a film called *Windtalkers* where it was a war movie. And we developed a fast way to do I made my dirt out of child's tempera paint and acrylic. So we could spray it on or have people run around and hit them with a sponge, blow dirt in their face, and send them out of the trailer.

And Connie Nielsen, a beautiful woman, had to have a look of no makeup, but I still had put some makeup on her. So I just do washes of color on her. Let her freckles show through and sunburn her up. And her hair couldn't be too good if you remember her in *The Devil's Advocate*. And she came to this show, and she's not getting much, but she was great. She stuck with it and accepted the part the way it was. I remember Michael Chiklis had an allergic reaction to alcohol, and if he smelled alcohol, his throat would tighten up. And he couldn't breathe. And the normal way we would do makeup using our apple-based palates is to spray alcohol into the palate, dip it with a sponge, and dab it on. Well, that is what created it. But we found out that if we airbrushed it, it would evaporate before it was hidden. So, we would run everyone through with an airbrush and hit them quickly. So we streamlined that quickly. Because they would, you know, typically you do all your wide stuff. First, we could always tweak them and make them suitable for close-ups later. And they had, you know, goggles and a lot of things on. So, you know, the makeup itself was general, and I tried to make it as easy as possible because I knew we had, at times, a lot of other stuff that was going to prohibit us from spending a lot of time in the makeup chair with certain people.

It was interesting because everyone...we had all the soldiers completely clean-shaven the whole time, like, they took a shot of something that didn't make them get beard stubble. We were creating a fantasy film, and that worked. Gary Busey was an interesting guy when he showed. I'd worked with Gary before. A long time ago, I made my bones with Gary. And I chased him around Atlanta, Georgia, doing him in age makeup. That's not an easy thing to do. But when I heard Gary would be on the show, I went to the script reading just to say hi and made a lot of noise on the show. Gary had been through a motorcycle accident a couple of years before. So, he had this funny thing with his eye, which would tear up a lot. And I looked at Gary and thought, if I do a really cool like, looks like an old burn like you got shocked by lightning. You know, a weird spidery scar in a big strip of white in your hair. I thought that he liked it. He loved it. So Gary would come in, I would put a little base on him airbrush his thing on whitening his hair, and he was out, and he was kind of interesting character.

Dennis Liddiard and I did Kurt's daily makeup together as he had a prosthetic above one eye and several small scars. Once I had the eyepiece in place and the scars positioned, I would step away, and Dennis would carry on finishing Kurt and maintaining him throughout the day. I would then take care of Connie Nielsen, Jason Scott Lee, Gary Busey, and other characters. Peter Handled Jason Isaacs, Sean Pertwee, and other characters. Dennis, when available, he pitched in when he could. Makeup artist Mark Landon covered the second unit and worked with us on many of our stunt players and additional cast.

Barney Burman worked with me in my lab sculpting, moulding, preparing prosthetics, and helping on set on occasion. Makeup Artist Greg LaCava also joined us for a portion of shooting and an array of other talented makeup artists on big days. Fred Blau also produced our tattoos for us. The hair department head was Peggy Semtob, joined by other hairstylists, Carolyn Elias, Janis Clark, and Sue Maust.

On Jason Issacs's character and cut death scene:

Jason wanted to do cool stuff. I hit this little pencil-thin Mustache. It was this tiny lace little Mustache to get him that Clark Gable thing, and if it was off, it was off, you know. So, he was meticulous about it. He comes from the theatre in England. So, he was particular about certain things. He brought something nice to the table, and he looked at things, and we had to do a thing where it was cut from the film where his head exploded because he's trying to deactivate a bomb. In the very last scene, they want to combine effects shot digital with a practical effect.

I made a prosthetic head. When it was made up, I had a generic head, and the hair was put on, the eyes read it, the mustache was on it, it resembled Jason, and the head was screaming. So, I made this head up, painted it up, and then we put it on a rig where there's a skull inside. So, if you score the face and push, the face would pull back and reveal this bloody skull. It's almost like the skin peeling off in the face. It had to be very rapid, and we fixed it up on a rig, and I looked at this thing for like two weeks in the trailer and went to shoot it, and I cut this whole thing up and did the rig, and they shot the same. And I don't think they filmed it enough or adequately because sometimes the director or the camera department thinks they know how something should look. But they don't have any idea about the effects side of things. Their approach was to fix it in digital later.

Famous last words, and the scene never really made. It didn't fit in. Because it was just a moment where he looks up and the numbers go from 01 to zero and explosion. They wanted that that split second like that. I never saw the footage. I don't even know whatever became of it if it ever existed.

Following pages have the Makeup rundown that Steve LaPorte prepared for the Academy.

SOLDIER

- MAKEUP -

When creating the makeup for "Soldier" several factors had to be addressed. First, a Military look for the Soldiers & Officers. Second, a dusty windblown look for the Settlers of the "Garbage Planet". And third, a "no makeup" look for everything. Somewhat of a contradiction in terms but with the use of ***transparent airbrush colors & translucent materials for prosthetics*** along with careful use of ***earthtone bases*** I feel that our department did quite well under the shooting conditions.

For Jason Scott Lee As "Caine 607" I chose to use Gelatin prosthetics for his eye wound & aftermath scarring. I then designed a contact lens to give his eye a scarred & dead look. Originally the Director wanted his eye to be covered with the scar but the final fight sequence required a great deal of Martial Arts type fighting on uneven terrain. I felt that blinding our actor in one eye would be unsafe & restricting so the use of the lens proved very effective visually & still allowed Jason full freedom.

In the case of Kurt Russell as "Todd" we used a total of 5 plastic appliances & a gelatin "boxers eye" piece over his left eye. A large scar across his right eye, chin, nose, forehead & ear scars gave him the look of a battle worn Soldier. At times when exposed, body scars of various shapes & sizes were added to complete his look. We were under strict restraints by the Producers not to hide their "Star" behind the makeup , yet at the same time Kurt drove us to push the limit. Although subtle the gelatin piece over his eye proved to be so effective in altering Kurt's features throughout shooting most of the crew including the D.P. did not realize he had it on. Paired with the disfiguring scar on his other eye & the other small facial scars Kurt had a totally believable look.

Having worked with Gary Busey before I knew that he had limited patience in the chair so I turned to my Airbrush for help. Using a combination of 3 shades I added a marbling of colors on his cheek, temple & neck in order to achieve an old "acid burned" scarred effect. I then added a white strip of color in his hair to give him that "struck by lightening" look. More painted scarring around his eyes & nose & a light base to tie it all together got him out of the chair in less than 20 min. yet created a truly believable character. Again, I had people coming up to me on set & asking me if Gary really looked that "bad".

In the case of Connie Nielson, I used a staining technique of burnishing in a dark earthtone base & contouring & shading with other shades & powders to get a windblown yet Beautiful & a "no makeup" look.

The rest of the cast including all the children were run through the makeup trailer for a weathered look & this is where the Airbrush again kept us on time & efficient in our task. A reddish Tattoo shade was applied & then a brownish shade. Then several shades of powders were applied to get that "ground in dirt" look.

In every case the makeups had to hold up for long shooting days & for many scenes ,"pouring rain". In which case for our final fight sequence between "Todd" & "Caine 607" became a very difficult maintenance challenge for continuity. Gelatin appliances in the rain can become a real nightmare but proper prep & sealing of the pieces along with constant blotting after every take kept them intact for the 2 week sequence. Running blood was another problem. I formulated a "blood Pax" & a tattoo blood color to match all of the pre established bleeding & then Blood gels & regular blood was then applied so during the take blood would seem to flow without completely washing away.

In several scenes Kurt wore camouflage makeup & in the final scene again the Producers wanted his face to be clear of too much makeup. Special attention had to be paid to a gradual loss of the camouflage throughout the fight & further battle scenes with the other Enemy Soldiers.

A tattoo of each Soldiers name, serial number & blood type had to be applied to every Soldiers face. The Soldiers numbered sometimes in excess of 40. Thanks to Computer graphics & Real Creations, Sheets of tattoos were premade & applied using 99% alcohol. A custom assortment of 10 scare plates were made to produce the 100's of scars necessary to keep up with Kurt, Jason & quite often makeups we had to pull out of our hats at the request of the Director.

Our Makeup Dept. included Myself, Peter Montagna (my 2nd), Dennis Liddiard (Kurt Russell's personal Mkup.),Mark Landon, & Greg LaCava.
Our Hair Dept. was headed by Peggy Semtob with Janis Clark, Sue Maust & Carolyn Elias.

Thank You for your consideration.

Sincerely, Steve LaPorte

Banned From The Ranch Visual Effects

Visual Effects and Computer Graphics company Banned from the Ranch provided 19 keys visual effects shots for *Soldier*. One of the first tasks for the Banned from the Ranch team was to design and composite various futuristic computer screens into live-action production footage. During filming, it hadn't been made, so viewscreens and monitors on the sets were backlit green.

The screens, which ranged from navigational monitors, targeting screens, countdown timers, and proximity alerts, were designed by visual effects supervisor Van Ling and animated by graphic artist Ian Marks. The slick screens needed to convey detailed information that the characters required to comprehend and the audience. The film's resolution screens were created in Adobe Photoshop and animated in Adobe After Effects, with some 3D elements created in ElectricImage.

Once the graphics were designed and created, they composited the screens into the anamorphic production footage for a dozen shots, which required accurate, frame-by-frame tracking, rotoscoping, and compositing supervised by 2D supervisor Todd Vaziri and executed by artists Martha Soehendra and Josh Saeta using after-effects.

For one particular shot, the camera began with the monitor screen nearly filling the frame; as the shot progressed, the camera dollies back to reveal the soldiers Todd and Riley looking at the monitor, which displays a galaxy map. Todd taps the screen with his finger to select a destination, opening a screen window with more data. The camera move wasn't shot motion-control, so the camera was bouncing all over the place. In addition, the screen faces were all oddly-shaped to get away from the traditional rectangular look, which made the tracking even more challenging. With the addition of raster lines, film grain, and monitor reflections, they could incorporate the graphics seamlessly into the scenes.

For the crawler vehicle display video monitor graphics and cockpit shots, Banned from the Ranch created and composited the monitor screens by a using a background plate that was provided by the production of a chrome console with a backlit green screen, to which the graphic readout was added.

Interview with Van Ling Visual Effects Supervisor

How did you end up in visual effects?

I've been a fan of visual effects and science fiction, fantasy, and all that kind of stuff since childhood, between the great Ray Harryhausen films and watching reruns of *Star Trek*. I was only two when that show first aired, so I was watching it in reruns in the early 1970s. And I was also into disaster movies, which, of course, means lots of visual effects and practical effects, miniatures, all that kind of stuff.

Back in those days, we had 8mm cameras for home movies, but I didn't even have a "modern" Super-8 camera as a kid; I had a regular 8mm wind-up camera, which is actually called "double-8mm" format; the film cartridges used 16mm film, and you would put the cartridge in, film for 25 feet on one half of the roll, take it out, turn it over, put it back in the other way, and shoot the other 25 feet, for a total of 50 feet, so that when you sent it off to develop it, they would split the 16mm film down the middle into two 8mm-wide strips; that's how they used to do that. I would work on trying to replicate (very poorly!) the effects that I'd seen in movies. So that's kind of how I got interested in it and was doing a little bit of stop motion with clay, crude double exposures, miniatures, and so forth.

And then, of course, *Star Wars* came out, and that changed everything for everybody, because all of a sudden it became this thing that wasn't just for a bunch of geeks who were in the margins; it opened up the doors and general acceptance, in a lot of cases. And so I ended up devouring all of that and every other film that came out in the late seventies to early eighties, graduated from high school in 1982, went to film school at USC, which was George Lucas' alma mater, and went through that whole program.

Then, in the summer of 1986, just after I graduated from USC Cinema School, I had the wildest opportunity of my life out of the blue simply because I wanted to do a Halloween costume based on the newly-released film *Aliens*. I made a Halloween costume of the power-loader just on my own because I loved *Aliens* so much. And I ended up catching Jim Cameron's attention. And that's kind of how my career started. He gave me my first opportunity to work on these amazing film projects starting on the ground floor because he came from this kind of background himself. Starting with *The Abyss*, I got to be his researcher and creative/technical assistant, not only for VFX but also for the storytelling aspects. At one point, he started calling me his "extra RAM" because I was helping keep track of both creative and logistical things for his projects. I got to go through a bunch of great movies with him, learning at the right hand of a master filmmaker.

Then I went off on my own to be a creative director for a little shop called Banned from the Ranch Entertainment (BFTR) with Casey Cannon, who was an ILM alum that had started this little boutique graphics company. She and I met on *T2* and hit it off, so I worked on a whole lot of films with her at BFTR, and that quantity was the difference from working on Jim's films.

Cameron's movies, of course, are huge, and they're amazing and fantastic, but because of that, they're all-consuming and you'd only do one show every two or three years; I worked with him for eight years, during which I think I only worked on four movies total. It's interesting. When I was thinking, "What should I do? Where am I going to go with my career," Jim suggested I should either go fully into hands-on computer graphics and maybe go work at DD and do visual effects. Or, if want to learn to direct, needed to spend more time working full-time on sets. The way to get set experience is to work on other shows. So, what I ended up doing was combining both of his suggestions: I went off and started working on shows that were learning to use computers for playback in real-time on set, for doing a lot of screen graphics. You'll see a lot of that kind of thing in *Soldier* that we did, because we ended up making a name for ourselves at Banned from the Ranch for doing screen graphics.

In the old days, computers seen in the movies were mostly just TV monitors with video playing on them pretending like they were computers, and the technology was very simple. It was just video playback. And people would make animated graphics and stuff on either real computers or animation stands, and output them to industrial-quality 3/4-ince videotape, and then play those tapes back on set to make it look like you're working on a computer. We were in this first wave of shows that started using real computers on set for playback. The first big show to do that was *Jurassic Park*, which I didn't work on. But I knew the folks who worked on that and we learned from them and then took over being the flagbearer for that area of expertise for a while. In *Jurassic Park*, for instance, they had all these computers in the control center as part of the set and storyline. And the big deal at that time was that it was all Silicon Graphics machines, which were product-placed the same way you do with cigarettes and cars and everything else. Silicon Graphics was the de-facto computer hardware company that had the super-powerful computers which were the go-to systems for creating computer graphics for VFX in everything from *Terminator 2* and *Jurassic Park* and so on. They decided as a company that they wanted to get their name out there as the top brand in high-end computing, so they made a deal with Universal Pictures and Amblin (Spielberg's company on *Jurassic Park*) to have their computers not only used to make the CG dinosaurs behind the scenes, but to have their hardware on the set with their logos prominently visible. It's kind of like doing product placement for Dell or Apple in the movies, and they did it as the basically one and only brute-force, giant high-end computer company.

So in *Jurassic Park*, you see Silicon Graphics machines supposedly used to run all the systems in the park, and they make a big deal about "This is Unix,

I know this," right? So that started a trend where all the studios wanted to product-place actual Silicon Graphics machines on the sets, and maybe we can use it to actually do playback with high-rate, higher-resolution graphics, and that was always the goal. Because when you use just normal TV video equipment as your monitor, it doesn't matter how big your monitor is, the actual image resolution was only 640 by 480 pixels, because that was standard definition video, at least in the United States. So the graphics never looked any better than that. But now, everybody was seeing that computers could do higher resolution than video, so it made sense that Silicon Graphics supercomputers should be able to handle this. And boy, we went through some real challenges with it.

Our first film using Silicon Graphics machines as product placement, on the heels of *Jurassic Park*, was Frank Marshall's film *Congo* in 1995, which we shot in '94. And it was really interesting, because in those days you had to find a way to adjust the colour on the computer video monitors so they didn't always come out looking very blue on film. When you see them on-screen, computer monitors are always cold-looking, because of the colour temperature of the rasters. Now, on normal TV video monitors, you had the ability to change radically change the colours and warm them up a little bit. Not so much with the computer screens; they were just what they were, with very little colour controls, and they were cold and not very bright. We were shooting with Allen Daviau, the cinematographer who did *E.T.*, and he wanted the computer screens to look natural and warm, where skin tones looked more normal. He didn't want any room with computer displays to be where everything's blue and then the whole set lighting also has to be all blue to make things match, and so we had to come up with ways of adjusting the computer monitors which really weren't designed to be able to change their colour temperature much, and try to make them so that they look more natural.

On top of that, we had to help tell the high-tech story in the film by creating all these screen graphics. I love doing screen graphics and we created a whole bunch of things, multi-screen windows and interfaces. One of the things we found that was killing us was that if we wanted to have a normal standard-TV-resolution video image fill the entire screen of a Silicon Graphics computer monitor that, as opposed to a video like a television monitor, the Silicon Graphics machines couldn't easily do it, not despite having the capability of displaying four times that resolution, but actually *because* of it! They didn't work like a regular TV and blow up the image to fill screen; they could only play it in a 640 by 480 window, which drove us crazy, because the SGI processors weren't designed for simple video scaling on their screens. We had to figure out technically how to do that. And since we were building all of our graphics on Macintoshes—I've been a Mac guy forever—we would design the screens, break them down into modules, port the graphic components and stuff to the Silicon Graphics machines running the Irix OS. We had to work with these little UNIX utility programs that would display stuff and get them to try to figure out how to play these images and animations back. And we could never play full video! It drove us crazy, and it drove the people at Silicon Graphics crazy, because it makes perfect sense; we want to see an image full screen, you know, like a normal video image, but they said, "Well, we really can't do that. Sure, we can play it back in real time, but it's going to be regular TV-resolution window that will fill only a quarter of our high-resolution screen," because the time and processing calculations it took to scale it up for that particular Unix architecture was apparently very, very difficult. So it was really kind of kind of a funny that the highest quality, highest speed systems couldn't play something very simple and that was because they had the brute force to be able to do all the calculations and put things on the screen and do real time, move things around, take objects and rotate them. They used to do that. You see some of those things in *Jurassic*, I think. But playing back a video is not really their forte, whereas the quote unquote consumer-end computers like Macs and PCs didn't have the brute force CPU power that the SGIs did.

So, they had to come up with shortcuts, and those shortcuts are what made it possible to put things full screen. We figured out later that it would have been easier to texture map the video footage onto a flat 3D plane and zoom in on it to fill the screen, and that would have worked better! It was this really weird, topsy-turvy thing, but it was really cool trying to explore new ground. We ended up being the company that everybody hired to do computer playback, as opposed to just normal video playback, which we also did at BFTR before we also started doing straight-up visual effects shots as well.

So, I ended up working on movies like *Congo*, *Twister*, *Dante's Peak*, and *The Relic* using high-end SGI computers, and doing a lot of featured, story-critical graphics, which was really fun. When you're doing graphics, it's one thing to have a bunch of whizzy things going on the screens in the background just to show off that you're in a computer lab. The shows that we worked on were specifically about science or about scientists who were using the technology to advance the plot and be part of the story. So, for *Twister*, for instance, ILM was going to be doing these fantastic tornado simulations and visual effects shots, but nobody could afford to hire ILM to do that throughout the movie. So what that meant was the story was designed to kind of be like *Jaws*, where you only see the shark in the big climactic scenes. In the meantime, though, you're seeing the traces of it, the hints of it, the shadows of it, like with the yellow barrels. And those were what we were creating on the computers for the tornadoes and volcanos and so on. We had to be able to substitute in for the real deal by being the tracks or footprints, if you will, of the main creature or force of nature. And we had to have the actors be able to sit there and stare at screens and go, "Oh, my God, it looks like it's coming towards us!" And we have to create a graphic that gives that impression. So, it was really great, because we were really part of the storytelling. It was like, "Okay, what do we need to see here? The script says they see this event is happening." And then, additionally, our job was to say, "Okay, in real life, if we want to make this realistic, how would it look? How would the fictional scientific sensors and displays show it?" So, one of my favourite parts of doing these movies was the research, because I would go hang out with the National Severe Storms Laboratory people in Oklahoma and talk about tornado warning indicators. Or I would walk the lava flows in Hawaii with the USGS volcanologists to learn about how they study and monitor volcanic activity, and what their data screens and graphics would look like.

My favourite trick was to say, "Okay, if computers could do or show anything, what would you want them to be able to do for real for your scientific specialty?" They'd say "Well, we want to be able to monitor these gases and these kinds of tremors and have a screen that would show us these things." Then I would go and try to design that so that it wasn't just telling the story for an audience, but to have volcanologists, bacteriologists, and meteorologists hopefully look at it and go, "that's pretty accurate, and I wish we had that software for real." So that was the fun part.

So we did that for quite a while, and then we also did some kind of more science fiction-fantasy kind of graphics. For *Starship Troopers* and *Soldier*, we had different asks from each director as to what they wanted to see on the screens. For instance, we ended up replacing the people who originally were doing the *Starship Troopers* screen graphics because they made it look very realistically military for the time, which meant that there was really no visual graphics; there's just a lot of blocks of tiny green-on-black text information going by. It's interesting that *Starship Troopers* is kind of like "Soldier" in the fact that as a movie it was kind of ahead of its time; it wasn't appreciated as much when it first came out, because people were like, "I'm expecting a big space adventure. What the heck is this?" The whole FedNet thing, which was one of the things we did at BFTR for the show, with all the "Would you like to know more?" stuff, people are stomping on bugs as a way of being patriotic; big propaganda shots with bold lettering and all this craziness. Many people didn't get it, or they took it too seriously. They were like, "I don't like this. It's kind of almost making fun of us." It was only years later that it was appreciated for what it was doing. And, unfortunately, now years later, it's actually like that in America. It's very relevant, and the film was very prescient. *Soldier* was an interesting deal for that kind of thing as well. They wanted to make it very gritty. But *Soldier* was a different case for us, because we weren't involved in the shooting of it at all; we were brought in during post-production to do all our work.

Truth be told, I didn't mind coming onto films in post-production sometimes, because being on set and having to try to get all the computers working was a stressful pain in the neck. I went through that on *Twister*, where we were out on location in Oklahoma, needing to wrangle computers that had to work inside overheating, moving cars. The biggest problem there was that you can't see *any* computer screen if you're outside or in bright sunlight, as anybody who has tried to use a laptop or an iPad out in daylight would know: you can't see a damn thing because the screens just aren't bright enough. And so you have to do things like put like 12ND neutral density filters on the windshield just to bring down the brightness coming in through the glass enough that you could register an exposure of what's on the computer without everything outside being just blown-out white. It was a really interesting set of challenges, that and having working desktop computers driving LCD screens inside fake laptop shells, out in muddy fields where we have to run electrical power and ridiculously-long data cables all the way back to a generator and the desktops on rickety folding tables just out of frame, while they're dropping ice-cube-sized pieces of hail on us during the scenes. Computers don't really like that heat or abuse.

So, I was fine to do more shots in post. And, of course, nowadays all computer screens for the most part are done in post. They're just blank screens or green screens with tracking markers on them, and then people add the graphics in as visual effects composites. It's part of that whole "we'll do it in post, because we haven't designed it yet" kind of problem that the industry tends to pendulum through sometimes; it's like, "Oh, we can do everything using green screen now, we don't have to do anything for real, and it's safer and cheaper." Then it swings back towards "we're gonna do this stunt for real, we're not gonna do it all green screen because people appreciate it when they see a real stunt, real action, real screen graphics, so it doesn't just feel like everybody's just reacting to nothing." Screen graphics went through the same thing, where we did all of our pre-planning, designing and creation of all the graphics, and they told a story and you'd be on set. And the actors would respond to them, but they still wouldn't know how to use a keyboard and would frantically be pressing buttons, as if typing faster means that they're hackers! The benefit of actually putting things on the screens in the sets is that you get more interaction and reflection and colour changes from the screens on your actors and the sets; it gave them things to react to and the camera could actually get a two-shot of an actor over-the-shoulder with the graphic as opposed to staring at nothing and pointing to an area of a blank screen where something would be added in post— and he would be able to see what's going on and act more realistically to it. For a while, that kind of went away because it became easier to just track everything in later and people could figure out what they're going to put in later. But now the pendulum is swinging back just a little bit, I think, where it's at least a hybrid of people doing graphics on the set so you can see what was going on, and ideally the screens could be directed by the filmmakers in terms of timing information reveals based on the interaction with the actors. Because people who did playback on set for computers are pretty much now congruent with the people who do visual effects, it means that you can hire somebody to design the visual effects or the screens, and they can either play them back on set for best performance interaction, and if they end up having to change or redesign the screens for editorial reasons, they can also do the composites in post-production. That's the boutique niche BFTR fell into for a little while in terms of doing screen graphics, playback, and visual effects work.

With *Soldier*, they shot the film in 1997, which means we worked on it during post in 1998. And what was interesting there is our only contact with the show was essentially with the editorial department and Ed Jones, the visual effects supervisor, whom we kind of knew —he was an acquaintance of Casey's from her ILM days, and we had started making a name for ourselves doing some graphics stuff; storytelling graphics, not just wallpaper graphics, so that we can do both. And so they asked us to do some close-up screen graphic shots for them. I think the crawler screens might have been some of the first bits of graphic that we did. If you watch the film, you'll notice they had some graphics on set, but they were just basically transparencies, backlit transparencies, very military. They wanted to have stuff that would specifically tell the story points that they needed to do to give them editorial coverage, and that's one of the things we love doing, the storytelling process of it. It's like, "Okay, we see him looking at the screen, and then he says something about this. What is he going to see that'll help tell that story and make it clear to the audience what's going on?" It was just like with *Twister*, where if we can show a graphic that tells the audience how the two crawlers are on a collision course, then they don't have to pay for an expensive visual effect or practical shot of the real thing. So, we did the crawler graphics and kind of made it look like that videogame *BattleZone*. It's always this balance between how realistic you want to make it and how video game-like you want to make it, because those things are becoming more and more the same and ubiquitous to some extent.

***Soldier* was a huge production. When you look at the scale of it, it was phenomenal. I like how the beginning of the film starts the exposition with where it starts in his life, then you flesh, his training, and then through the wars, and it's done in such a way that it sets up the character. It's in a short space of time, but done so well.**

Well, that was the interesting thing about that show. If we come onto the show in post, we get to be surgical and efficient for the narrative. It's more a matter at that point of "we just need to do these specific things." Editorially, we need inserts; we need a specific insert shot that tell us this story point graphically, because we are trying to cut the time down, and we can't show this whole thing. But we could do it in a graphic, a heads-up display or screen, that will tell us everything the audience needs to know and not have to show four different shots of other things to get the point across. You've heard the phrase that "editorial is the final rewrite of a film," and it's true. I'm an editorial guy. I love editing, and I love how the storytelling process works and to see what you can do and what you can get away with in how you cut the picture and use the sound mix. It's like, "We're getting rid of this whole scene. How do we do this?" Well, sometimes you can do one good ADR line and it'll fulfil the exact same function as a three-minute scene. That's one of the things I learned; when you're telling a story and you have to cut things down, and you have to figure out how the scenes flow. So I love the fact that they were basically coming to us to help them solve this narrative problem. We need to flow over this little piece of this, and we want to do it with graphics, because it makes sense, because half of the storytelling can take place in the graphics and on the people. It's all visual, and so we got to be in part of that process of the storytelling, which is fantastic.

What was interesting on *Soldier* was that I never got to meet the director, Paul W.S. Anderson; I never met Kurt Russell; I never met anybody. I think I only went to the editorial offices once. It's no different than the way we work from home offices nowadays, but what we were given was, for instance, "Okay, here's a plate we shot for the crawler. We have this kind of viewing sight with this long, thin green-screen portion, and we need to fill that in with graphics. We've got it cut into the scene in a couple different places, and we're trying to get across this specific info in each cut." And they would give us a short video of just that edited sequence.

We never saw the whole movie until the crew screening. And I don't recall ever getting the script either, because we were just one of the minor visual effects houses that were brought in during post. We only did 19 shots on the show. Rhythm & Hues and Rainmaker, those guys were the big visual effects houses on the film. We were a support team, which was perfectly fine, because we still got to influence the story. The other nice thing is that you know if you're working on shots in post, they're probably going to be in the movie. Because some of them were envisioned only in post because they're trying to solve a narrative problem, or an editorial problem, or a time problem. If you need to get from point A to point B, we can give you exactly that, as opposed to when you're just working with editorial footage that you shot on the day on the set in production, during principal photography. It's like, "This almost tells it. It'll work for now, but wouldn't it have been great if we had footage of this, if it ended on this look as opposed to that look?" Or, "We don't have any takes that show that, but we have something that's close enough to get the point across." And with graphics in certain instances, we now have the ability to fix things and help better tell the story.

On the legacy of *Soldier* and genres:

Soldier has almost become something of a cult film. I think that some of these films don't get appreciated, because people sometimes have this attitude of "well, these are B pictures; they're just horror, shock, gore, fantasy, or science fiction." They look down on it. Because traditionally, the various genres were kind of split up and silo'd: there are prestige drama pictures, there's some wacky comedy and romance stuff, there is the science fiction and fantasy geek stuff, and those were all considered separate where none the twain shall meet. But that's no longer true. Because you have shows like *The Lord of the Rings* that can win a bunch of Oscars, or *The Shape of Water*. *Aliens* was a science fiction action movie that was nominated for seven Oscars, including Best Actress, so there are times when that kind of thing can happen.

I think that nowadays, you can blend things together, and just because it's mostly in a particular genre, it doesn't mean it should be relegated to just B-picture status. And that makes a huge difference when what people now want to do is to say, as Paul W.S. Anderson did, "You know, I want to do a haunted house movie set in space." Then later, with *Soldier*, he basically took *Shane*, the Western, and set it in space. So when you can mix the genres, it can broaden your audience and makes it kind of easier to take what some people might consider trash, other people consider a guilty pleasure, and yet other people who just revel in it, and make it a uniting kind of thing. *Star Wars* certainly did that. People can enjoy it without having to be ashamed of enjoying it, and we can all find more common ground.

In light of recent events, those films are relevant now, especially with Afghanistan and all this crazy stuff that keeps going on. *Soldier* remains relevant, even though it was made it was made pre-911.

I think that Paul W.S. Anderson took the idea of, "We're in America, where we're already considered kind of the World Police"; before T*eam America*. He said, "What if you extrapolated military efficiency to its logical conclusion? Building a better soldier, instead of just the *Robocop* kind of augmentation? What if you bred them and indoctrinated them?" The whole question of humanity or the lack thereof, or trying to breed and train it out of people. What I found really interesting, which wasn't a defined thing back when *Soldier* came out, but it is now, is the fact that it's really about PTSD. It's about the notion of how does somebody trained to kill all the time go about protecting civilians, yet be willing to shoot through them if necessary for the mission? And how do you reintegrate back into civilian society when you're finished serving?

You read stories now about people who come back, and the only way they can feel safe is they won't sleep in their bedrooms, they will sleep every night in a hole they've dug in the backyard. I mean, there are real cases that are that extreme. So the film now has a relevance that it didn't have acknowledged before. Because what was almost like fantasy, like, "Oh, this is too far, it will never happen like this." And then it happens like that. And that's exactly what you have today.

They become institutionalized. That's all they can do, and of course, what you say. it touches on it perfectly, because he's tossed away, like so many of these soldiers are when they come back home.

They fight and die and get maimed for their country. And when they come back, sometimes they get spit on. We went through all of that with Vietnam in the early 70s, here in the States. That was a period I grew up in. It's really interesting to see how, as the culture has changed, a movie that was marginalized or dismissed—I can't believe it only has a 13% rating on Rotten Tomatoes—can suddenly be prescient and acquire more meaning and relevancc. I think if more people watched it today, they probably say, "Hey, you know what? This is a surprisingly good film." I certainly felt that way when we watched the crew screening. We thought, this is a really good film, Kurt Russell's fantastic, and I was always joking that this is his *Terminator*, since he doesn't say more than 100 words in the show!

I go back now, and I look at the films that I kind of maybe dismissed earlier in my experience, and usually you'll find there are things that are worthy of merit. I hope that happens with *Soldier*, because there's a lot of good stuff in there. Kurt's performance is emotional with almost no dialogue. It's all visual. And I love the fact that he calls everyone, including Connie Nielsen, "sir." Of course, for me, that immediately echoed the relationship between Peppermint Patty and Marcie in the *Peanuts* comics, because Marcie always calls Peppermint Patty "sir," which is kind of funny and sad at the same time. Or perhaps that's just an American thing.

I also listened to the entire commentary that Paul W.S. Anderson , Jeremy Bolt, and Jason Isaac did. Apparently, Kurt broke his ankle a couple of weeks into the shoot, which is really funny that you mentioned *Terminator* being one of David People's inspirations, because Linda Hamilton sprained her ankle really badly while shooting the film, and they had to completely rearrange the filming schedule because she couldn't do all that running down the street from the Terminator as he's driving the truck. It sounds a lot like what happened with Kurt!

I absolutely think that the most fun thing we did on *Soldier* was to play with stuff on the screen and put Easter Eggs into the graphics. And one of the last shots I think we got on the show was to do this graphic to kind of cap off the whole montage of war scenes near the beginning of the film, where Kurt's going through and shooting people in that Moscow incident and all those things. They wanted us to do a shot where we see a kind of a digital dossier on Todd with his combat history. And they specifically said, "We consider this film to be in the same universe as *Blade Runner* because of David Webb Peoples being the screenwriter, and we have the iconic spinner vehicle in the film." And we actually did a VFX shot for the film where Todd gets knocked over by the sandstorm and we had to add digital debris and dust. We saw the sequence and I said, "Oh, yeah, that's a spinner. Nice." So we were asked to do this electronic dossier shot, and it was going to then transition to the shot of him sitting there with the graphic that says "Present Status: Between Wars."

I remember Ed Jones giving me specific instructions from the director. He wanted to make sure that the featured combat history section of the graphic includes the things that we have seen tattooed on Kurt's arm in the movie, some of the references to *Blade Runner*—Shoulder of Orion, Tannhauser Gate, and so on. So when you see the shot, the first featured stuff is the combat history, and it's got the *Blade Runner* stuff and the Argentine moons and all these continuity references as the first six things of what Paul had asked for.

But then I had more space to fill because the shot pulls back longer and the text is constantly scrolling to reveal more text, and I'm like, "Okay, what else can I put in there?" And I just went nuts and geeked out. So, if you look at that shot under the combat history, the three final things under the ones that were officially requested are actually references to *Star Trek II: The Wrath of Khan*. There's a point in that movie where Khan does this great speech, which is actually paraphrased from *Moby Dick*, about his obsession with Kirk: "He tasks me. He tasks me, and I shall have him. I'll chase him 'round the moons of Nibia and 'round the Antares maelstrom and 'round Perdition's flames before I give him up!" So I took those three things and I put them in as battles listed in Todd's combat history. So if you're a *Star Trek* fan, you'll catch those in there. And then the rest of it was, "Okay, if I'm doing *Star Trek* references, what else can I do here and have some fun with my fellow SF TV/movie fans?"

So I started putting more geek references in the graphics: I put in weapons shout-outs for the video game *Doom*; I put in a Marvin the Martian *Looney Toons* reference, since Warner Bros. made the movie; there's a laser bolo, which is a reference to the original *Battlestar Galactica*; and, of course, the M-41A pulse rifle and the smart guns from *Aliens*. And there's an obscure, deep cut reference to an old American west coast local radio station gag that mentioned a "Montgomery Ward T-2000 semi-automatic revolver, which, of course, makes no sense. I put all that in there as part of Todd's ordnance training. And then I started doing the commendations section and put in wacky references to various characters that Kurt Russell had played in his previous movies: the O'Neil Ring Award, the Captain Ron Trophy, the Dexter Riley Award, the McCaffrey Fire Award, the Plissken Patch, the Cash Medal of Bravery, and the MacCready Cross. I was just having way too much fun!

So I love putting in Easter Eggs and giving folks reason to look harder or watch things more than once and see if you can find them. And it's kind of like sending a hidden message that says, "Hey, if you get this, we're in your tribe. We are geeks and fans, just like you." And it was a gamble, because I didn't actually know Paul W.S. Anderson at all. But from his request to include the *Blade Runner* references, as far as I could tell, he seemed to be as much of a movie fan as I was. So I turned in the finished shot with all this crazy stuff hidden in it, and I remember thinking, "Uh-oh, they're gonna get mad at me," and "is this going to pull viewers' attention away from the narrative?" Then I get the word back that Kurt saw it and loved it. I think they even mentioned it in the DVD commentary, just pointing it out. So I'll take that as an affirmation and a compliment. So yeah, I love doing those kinds of things.

There are hidden references in other graphics as well. If you look at the Trinity Moon graphic at the end, in the search results on the right-hand side of the screen, there are more references to other shows: the Anoat system from *The Empire Strikes Back;* a Kessel reference to *Star Wars;* Planet

10 from *Buckaroo Banzai;* plus three separate references to *The Hitchhiker's Guide to the Galaxy*: Slartibartfast, Ursa Minor Beta, and ZZ9 Plural Z Alpha. And "Eminiar 7 NGC 321" is a reference to an original *Star Trek* TV series episode called "A Taste of Armageddon." So yeah, I tended to go overboard with my geekdom. Sometimes it works, and at worst goes unseen. Nowadays, people are used to this kind of thing because of Marvel and all of the film folk who grew up with all these common and sometimes not-so-common references in their lives. And it's also reinforced by video games, since the objective of a lot of gaming is to explore and find hidden things. So more people actually include and look for them now in movies and shows, which maybe kind of dilutes the specialness of Easter Eggs, but it's also something fun to do,. And in a way, if other people are appreciating these Easter Eggs, maybe they're also understanding the kind of love that science fiction fans have had for these shows and these worlds. In a lot of cases, we do them as tributes to the things we like or that influenced and inspired us. They're little shout-outs from one fan to another, which creates this moment of solidarity, you know? So as long as what's now called "fan service" doesn't pull people out of the show and distract from the storytelling, it's a fun thing to try to do.

Memories with Bret Bahe Building The Crawler

"I worked on those crawlers for about four weeks. The movie was fun, and it was fun to be part of a monumental production. I didn't design anything we just had drawings and we created what was on the drawing." (Trivia: The crawlers are based on *mining haul trucks*)

"Soldiers deserve soldiers, sir"—An Analysis of Soldier's Story, Theme, and Characters

The film began in 1996. From the very opening of *Soldier*, there is an introduction to the theme of dehumanization and Darwin's Theory of Natural Selection. The Adam Project gets initiated. It is a rigorous military training program where babies are taken and trained by the Army from birth. The children get exposed to bloody violence at a young age and are then encouraged to show strength—and no mercy—even to one another. They study tactics and train to be physically superior. The greatest of the Adam Project soldiers is Todd, played by Kurt Russell, a soldier who fights multiple successful campaigns, including the War of the Six Cities, the Moscow Incident, and the Argentine Moons War.

"The physicality of the movie is really the least interesting thing to me. It's Todd's mentality that's interesting. Todd and the other veteran soldiers have been raised in a military environment. The way these soldiers are raised—taken from a nursery, inducted into the military, and raised without exposure to love or other human emotions—is really the ultimate form of child abuse." [13]- Kurt Russell Soldier depicts a world built on militarism. On the [14]DVD commentary track, director Paul W.S. Anderson is open about the influence *Blade Runner* had on the project. "I always saw the movies as existing in the same universe *Blade Runner*, which is about the machine that becomes as human as it possibly can be, while this movie is about a man who

[13] *Starlog Magazine, Issue 258, page 33 (1998)*

[14] *Soldier DVD/BLU RAY Audio Commentary — Director Paul W.S. Anderson - Warner Bros. (1998)*

becomes as machine-like as the military can make him. So, in a way, they're both looking for their humanity."

The movie takes the tropes and conventions of film Westerns from the 1950/60s and transplants them into a futuristic setting. The most obvious example of the Western trope appearing in *Soldier* is the lone gunfighter coming to the rescue of people against injustice and evil, a Western motif that we have seen repeatedly. Todd 3456, played by Kurt Russell, is characterized in the mold of grizzled gunfighter characters like those played by John Wayne, Gary Cooper, and Clint Eastwood, and most specifically Alan Ladd in the 1953 Western *Shane*.

Kurt Russell is no stranger to the genre. He has played many anti-heroes and archetypal Western characters. These films include *Escape from New York* (1981), *The Thing* (1982), *Big Trouble in Little China* (1986), *Tombstone* (1993), *Stargate* (1994), *Escape from L.A.* (1996), *Bone Tomahawk* (2015), and *The Hateful Eight* (2015). One of Russell's heroes since boyhood was John Wayne, whose influence you can see in many of the performances he has given. In *Soldier*, the combat history of Kurt Russell's character, Todd 3465, has many sci-fi references and references, as well as references to other Kurt Russell films.

These references include:

- The battles of Tannhäuser Gate and Shoulder of Orion (references to *Blade Runner*)
- Receipt of the "Plissken Medal" (reference to *Escape from New York* and its sequel, *Escape from L.A.*).
- Receipt of the "O'Neil Ring Award" (reference to *Stargate*)
- Receipt of the "Cash Medal of Honor" (reference to *Tango and Cash,* 1989)
- Receipt of the "Maccready Cross" (reference to *The Thing*)
- Receipt of the "Capt. Ron Trophy" (reference to *Captain Ron,* 1992)
- Receipt of the "McCaffrey Fire Award" (reference to *Backdraft,* 1991)
- Receipt of the "Dexter Riley Award" (reference to *The Strongest Man in the World,* 1975, *Now You See Him, Now You Don't,* 1972, and *The Computer Wore Tennis Shoes,* 1969)
- Citations for the Nibian Moons Campaign, the Antares Maelstrom War, and the War Of Perdition's Flames (locations are references to *Star Trek II: The Wrath of Khan,* 1982).

The film also has an arching theme of old versus new technology. Colonel Mekum introduces a new group of genetically-engineered soldiers. Although it is never mentioned, these are supposed to be the Nexus replicants from the *Blade Runner* universe as this film is linked to that franchise. They are designed with superior physical attributes, a complete lack of emotion, and absolute aggression. Like all scientific and technological advancements, Todd and his soldiers were destined to become obsolete. In this scene, we get a great sense that both Col. Mekum and Church see the soldiers as valueless commodities. These two characters are essentially playing adversarial war-games that can be viewed the same as any past or future events among governmental and military leaders across the world. It's almost a game of chess to them. A dick measuring contest, if you will. Todd is like a vintage Timex watch, and his replacement Caine is representative of the digital age—an advance model that will take the place of human labour.

Arcadia 237, the planet on which Todd is dumped, has potent metaphorical meaning for the film in which the tagline sums up "Left for dead on a remote planet for obsolete machines and people, a fallen hero has one last battle to fight." The character Todd's journey is representative of the stories in Greek mythology called Katabasis—the epic convention of the hero's trip into the underworld.

Todd moves through the terrain and passes through the sight of a crashed ship called Pandora. In Greek mythology, Pandora, who was not only the first woman, but an instrument of the wrath of Zeus, was held responsible for releasing the ills of humanity into the world. Todd soon discovers a colony, falls from a great height, and is knocked unconscious. He awakens to a golden hair beauty named Sandra. Connie Nielson, who plays Sandra, shares similarities with the beauty of Jean Arthur's character, Marian Starrett, in *Shane*. The name Sandra has a significant and spiritual meaning in the Bible. It means "the defender of mankind" or "she is brave." Nathan, her son's name is of Hebrew origin and means "gift of God." These characters make a fusion of progression in Todd's reawakening and understanding of humanity.

Sandra is a defender of Todd, and Nathan is the gift of God to Todd in his spiritual journey. Sandra and her husband, Mace, shelter Todd. Everyone knows that a *mace* was a medieval *weapon* used by knights, but his name also means gift Of God. Todd›s name means «fox,» and the name Fox means "wild animal in the dog family," which is very much like Todd. He is a wild animal-like pet taken in by this family. All this is something that not many have been noticed before, particularly at the time by critics, and is a whole new interpretation.

Later on, Todd is eating with the colonists and gets asked why he is not with his unit anymore. He states, "I was replaced." In *Soldier*, the process of advanced technological innovation is to demonstrate military superiority. The dictionary defines automation as "the technique of making an apparatus, a process, or a system operate automatically." We define automation as "the creation and application of technology to monitor and control the production and delivery of products and services." A new engineered soldier has replaced Todd. It drives home the meaning of existentialism and that Todd realizes that his existence was meaningless and redundant, but he slowly learns the freedom of choice and the responsibilities that go along with it. He becomes more aware of his options, freedom to make decisions, and the consequences of his actions. The time with the colony helps him develop a better sense that he is the "author" of his own life rather than be a slave to the corrupt capitalistic and militaristic machine that had discarded his life.

Soldier raises essential questions about how men get brutalized by war's violence and the impossibility of leaving that behind. *Soldier* is a lot more, and is a movie full of deeper subtext, such as the feelings which form between Todd and Sandra, plus the idolization of her son, Nathan. As such, *Soldier* is a movie which, to fully appreciate, you need to look at the layers below the well-used storyline of a mysterious stranger walking into a town. Below is a crucial scene and dialogue from *Soldier* with Sandra and Todd.

> Sandra: "Sgt. Todd... what's it like? What's it like being a soldier? What do you think about?"
>
> *[silence]*
>
> Sandra: "You must think about something?"
>
> *[silence]*
>
> Sandra: "What about feelings then?"
>
> *[silence]*
>
> Sandra: "You must *feel* something?"
>
> *[pause]*
>
> Todd: "Fear."
>
> Sandra: "Fear?"
>
> Todd: "Fear and discipline."
>
> Sandra: "Now?"
>
> Todd: "Always."

Todd takes a liking to Mace and falls for his wife, Sandra, and her son, Nathan. I also enjoyed the juxtaposition of the soldier dressed in his trench coat and trying to live a colonist's life, unable to understand or adjust to their way of life. He looks harmless one moment and the next extremely dangerous. These scenes examine war's unrelenting damage to the human psyche and how a soldier and individuals can be institutionalized. The character Todd has been living in a state of militarism for much of his life. He cannot live an independent life in the outside world. He has never been able to think and act independently, apart from following orders because of having lived under the rules of the military. The similarities between Todd and Alan Ladd's character in *Shane* are prevalent throughout the film. In a sequence involving Todd and Nathan, Todd teaches Nathan the necessary violence to protect himself. Nathan later uses what he learned to save his parent's lives. "Of course, there are parallels to SHANE. Nathan the little boy who's bitten by a viper, can no longer speak. He's very similar to Todd in that he's smart and he thinks, but he doesn't speak. But Nathan's been traumatized. In a way, he's a reflection in a symbolic way of a bit of a character who's like Todd in that he's been traumatized severely. And he's a creature of his environment. He finds Todd fascinating, much the same way the little boy found Shane fascinating." [15] - Kurt Russell

The colonists decided that Todd's background as a soldier and violent tendencies were such that he could not integrate into human society. He is abandoned and cast out of the community. It causes him to undergo a profound existential crisis, finding his sense of identity and humanity. He sheds a tear. It is a testament to Russell's underrated acting that he pulls this off with significant effect.

Todd has come off as an outsider, a loner who's not learned about human relationships over his 40-year career as a soldier and war-spanning existence until he realizes his life was stolen from him. You feel empathy and compassion for him, giving the film more texture and depth. *Shane* and *Soldier* have characters cut from the same cloth, with very similar personalities and individualistic loners. David Peoples, who wrote *Soldier,* also wrote the Oscar-winning *Unforgiven.* The latter film has a lot in common with *Soldier*, on a thematic level, the idea that killing leaves an imprint on one's soul that can never be erased. This quote Clint Eastwood's Munny character from *Unforgiven* best describes its connection with *Soldier* in character terms: "It's a hell of a thing, killing a man. You take away everything he's got and everything he's ever gonna have."

---

[15] *Cinefantastique Vol 20 No 9-10 November page 13 (1998)*

One of the unique elements of the film is the depth that the film gives both sides of the conflict. Sure, the film has shown the nature of what violence can do, but the last battle with the replicant soldiers was a celebration of righteous revenge in the best tradition of the classic Western. And it was consistent with Russell's *oeuvre*, culminating with a line worthy of iconic status: "I'm going to kill them all, sir!" (Trivia: One of the soldiers engaged in the raid on the Arcadia 234 settlement fires a minigun. The weapon has appeared in the films *Last Action Hero*, *Terminator 2: Judgement Day*, and *Predator*.) Todd kills the soldier when his minigun jams, then using it when engaging the soldiers following the raid. Todd's weapons training record lists the USMC Smartgun and the M41A pulse rifle, which are references to the weapons used in James Cameron's *Aliens*. There is a connection to the videogame *Doom* with the gun DOOM MKIV BFG. Also, Illudium PU36 Explosive Space Modulator is the same weapon Marvin the Martian constantly threatens to use on Earth in his Bugs Bunny cartoon appearances. In keeping with the style of the film, the guns used are anachronistic, giving the feeling of a throwback to the old-fashioned Western and calvary flicks. The film used many rifles, handguns, machine guns, shotguns, and a rocket launcher. A complete list of weapons used in the movie is below.

- M4A1 Carbine
- M16A2 Rifle
- M16A2 Rifle
- AKU-94 Bullpup
- Heckler & Koch HK91A2
- Claridge LEC9
- Norinco MAK-90
- Remington Rolling Block
- Rocky Mountain Arms Patriot Pistol
- Modified Winchester Lever Action Rifle
- Heckler & Koch Mark 23 pistol
- Colt Single Action Army - Colonel Mekum shoots Captain Church with this handgun.
- Astra 400
- Astra 400M60 Machine Gun

- Fake DShKs mocked up from Browning M2HBs – These can be seen early on in the film on the Humvee vehicles used by the military when they are watching the training of the young boys as Soldiers than later on by the new Soldiers on the crawlers.
- Minigun
- Heckler & Koch MP5A2
- Franchi LF-57 – Todd fires duel l LF-57s during "Battle of the Argentine Moons"
- Steyr SPP
- Valtro PM5 shotgun
- Tru Flite 37mm Super Long Range Gas Gun
- Heckler & Koch P2A1 Flare Pistol
- Rocket Launcher – Todd uses against one of new Soldiers
- Flamethrowers - Used by the new Soldiers on the attack of Arcadia

Although it might sometimes fall to the wayside in favour of visuals, sound is an equally important part of the film in its impact on enhancing the movie experience.

I think you could also view *Soldier* as using settler society as a storytelling device for a symbol of civilization. In the colonial settlement, some are later murdered just for being there. It was perhaps exploring the uncomfortable consequences of colonialism. So when the community faces annihilation at the hands of the same military machine that discarded Todd, he shows his former superiors just how deadly an obsolete warrior can be. There is a theme of Frankenstein's monster. Todd was the best soldier they ever created, and he has become their worst nightmare.

> "Caine is a creature of pure aggression, but he's not so much a villain, but an opponent. My character and Kurt's are equally good and bad. If the audience roots for both Caine and Todd, that's acceptable, because both characters are soldiers who are simply following orders. There's nothing evil about his intentions. Caine is just taking orders from his superiors. At the end, I suppose there's this sort of revenge factor that comes into play, but before that, I would have to say that Caine is equal parts good and bad." [16]
>
> — Jason Scott Lee

[16] *Starlog Magazine, Issue 255 (1998)*

The final fight between Todd and Caine is very much in the vein of the classic Western showdown. It is a spiritual and physical struggle fought in the rain, wind, and fire. It visualizes, allegorically, an ultimate fusion of elemental groups from which the psyche of these characters inhabits. They each share the same occupation. Todd ultimately finds a way to overcome the challenge posed by his replacement. Todd may be old, but he is not obsolete. With the exhaustion and sadness on Kurt Russell's face as he snaps his enemy's neck, he shows respect from one warrior to another.

Costume designer Erica Phillips is known for her work in such films as *Robocop*, *Total Recall*, and *In the Line of Fire*. Erica worked on *Soldier* and played an essential role in aiding the filmmakers. Like her previous work, it blends into the environment in *Soldier's* story. Todd's costume design transmits a blend of alienness to viewers, thereby interpreting that he was both from the world of militarism and then adjusting to a new life with the colonists. The costumes of the other characters of the movie, Church, Colonel Mekum, Caine 607, the colonists, and the new soldiers, were enough to identify viewers with the idea of light and darkness and not get them lost in the meaning of the costume.

David Tattersall was the cinematographer for *Soldier* and would later work on *Star Wars: Episode 1: The Phantom Menace*. Being that *Soldier* was filmed in contrast, the lighting and camera work were critical elements in capturing the audience and pulling them into the story. Tattersall's palette is dark and dystopian in the opening scenes, showing the soldiers as dehumanized stone-cold killers, with the lighting reinforcing the sense of inhumanity in this world. As the story progresses, it becomes more vibrant. It symbolizes Todd's gradual transformation; in the beginning, when he is nothing more than a killing machine, and then when he is castaway to the junk planet, he is starting his journey to becoming more human. There is a light at the end of the tunnel, in essence. Director of photography Tattersall and the lighting department imbue the lighting and colour grading that contributes enormously to the overall look of a film. It begins with icy blue colours and then with warmer sepia tones on the planet of Arcadia, and the film's finale is a collision of both.

At the end of *Soldier*, Todd has won the battle, and as he gets up, we see a flame behind him. The ultimate fusion of social identity that emerges as an expression of hellish chaos he wants to leave behind forever. This further points out that *Soldier* like *Unforgiven* and *Blade Runner* and takes place in a world of moral ambiguity. Heroes and villains in this world are flip sides of the same coin.

"One of the things that I think is cool about this movie is unbeknownst to anybody, is these old soldiers have formed a family. "True, it is without emotion, without the normal standard of interplay. They're like a pack of wolves, and Todd is the alpha dog." [17]- Kurt Russell

Todd reunites with his former comrades, and there is a great sense of camaraderie as they salute each other. A vital element of the film is the relationship between Nathan and Todd, which illustrates Todd's reawakening. This relationship embodies the film's ending with its deep emotion as they look into the galaxy of space.

Soldier is a movie that can be viewed purely as entertainment, but it is a movie where you need to read between the lines as to why Todd not only takes a stand for his new surrogate family and tries to gain his lost sense of what it is to be human. And it is when you read between the lines and look at the deeper subtext that it becomes more than just another science fiction/ Western and, indeed, something special.

---

[17] *Starlog Magazine, Issue 258 (1998)*

PKD flashback: Russell gives powerful turn in 'Blade Runner' sidequel 'Soldier' (1998) (Review)

by John Hansen

Although many *Blade Runner* fans are probably familiar with the references to Tannhäuser Gate in *Soldier*, I think this film – likewise written by David Webb Peoples — should be more embraced as part of the "BR" universe than it is. At three points in the film – once on a monitor showing Todd's (Kurt Russell) military campaigns, once as a tattoo on Todd's arm, and once verbally by Mace (Sean Pertwee) – the battle of Tannhauser Gate is referenced. And the Shoulder of Orion is also in Todd's files.

Thus, although we don't know the nature of those two battles, we do know that both Roy Batty (Rutger Hauer) — who mentions the battles in his "tears in rain" monologue — and Todd fought in them. We know they take place between 2015 and 2019, within the four-year lifespan of Roy Batty. That also lines up with Todd's military career; he would be in his prime at that point. So while *Soldier* is a tangential "Philip K. Dick movie" rather than a core entry, I think it qualifies as much as, for example, the *Screamers* sequel.

By 2036, the time of *Soldier's* events, Todd is considered obsolete, with the next iteration of lab-produced soldiers replacing Todd's naturally born, strictly-trained generation. While PKD rarely wrote about soldiers – instead preferring low-level bureaucrats – Todd is the PKD version of a solider if there ever was one. He's literally thrown out with the garbage; the military doesn't even go to the effort to check if he's still alive.

I'll forever be in the minority on this, but I loved *Soldier* in 1998 and still do today. Upon its theatrical release, I thought it was smart SF, influenced by my already high opinion of director Paul W.S. Anderson from the previous year's *Event Horizon.* I hope someday *Soldier* takes its deserved place as a cult classic alongside that space-horror gem.

Today, I admire *Soldier* as a window into the future of military operations (I would've said "warning" in 1998, but today it's simply a window), a dark comedy (it's hilarious how serious the tone is early on, and later on, the one-liners are delicious), a tasty revenge yarn, and a legitimately moving story – thanks to Russell, who shows so much depth within a narrow range of facial expressions.

In a pivotal scene on the garbage planet, Todd tries to teach young Nathan (Jared Thorne) how to kill a deadly snake by crushing its head with a boot. He's then kicked out of the camp. I think this sequence sums up the ideal audience for the film and explains why it wasn't a hit: *Soldier* is perfect for young people growing up in an age/culture wherein they need to learn the harsh lessons of life, when sheltering and coddling them would be a clear disservice. 1998 America was not that time and place, and maybe 2020 isn't either, but it might be coming.

Knowing that this movie is part of the *Blade Runner* universe is important for understanding why Arcadia 234 is a relatively nice place to live, despite being the place where humanity dumps its garbage. As Connie Nielsen's Sandra says, at least they are left alone here. If one thinks about the rainy, filthy 2019 Los Angeles of *Blade Runner* – filled with cop cars that literally look down on you, and where it can be lucrative to hunt down escaped slaves – it makes sense that "being left alone" would be a breath of fresh air, even if you're inhaling the stench of garbage.

Todd has never been left alone, so we see how a man would turn out after 40 years of "fear and discipline" being the only feelings he knows. Russell gives a tremendous performance in *Soldier;*witness how Todd tightens up when Sandra hugs him. It's been said that children are adaptable, and if Todd has had 40 years of forced childhood (in the sense of not being free to make his own choices), the remainder of *Soldier* is about him learning how to be human. An intrinsic sense of decency exists within Todd, and when given a chance, it emerges.

Obviously this exchange …

> Sandra: "But one soldier, against 17. What are you going to do?"
>
> Todd: "I'm going to kill them all, sir."

… is a ridiculous (yet pure and effective) crowd-pleaser that serves a purpose within the narrative and in getting people to see the movie, via its use in the trailer. That said, I don't think *Soldier* is a ridiculous movie on the whole. It's brazenly simple and unsubtle, yet it works on all the aforementioned levels and allows room for a viewer to insert their own metaphor. Heck, I can see *Soldier* as a metaphor for life—it's a series of beat-downs, but be on the lookout for the rare good things.

And Peoples gives *Blade Runner* fans a treat by opening up the universe, by suggesting who Batty's bunch might've been fighting in space, and by introducing new planets and moons. The two *BR* films and the novel, *The Edge of Human*, take place on Earth, and the novel *Replicant Night* stays within our solar system. Perhaps the impossible-to-find novel *Eye and Talon* goes to the stars. And that's one of the appeals of *Soldier* for a *Blade Runner* nerd. Even if it's a garbage planet, I'll take it.

Rating 4.5

Soldier (1998): Coming to Terms with Your Past (a.k.a. Healing Your Inner Child)

by Mark Stratton

When I watch movies, I tend not to pay much attention to production brilliance or mistakes made by the people who created it. Okay, yes, sometimes I'm really picky, but I mostly judge movies or TV shows based on how they make me feel. If a movie makes me feel uncomfortable or disturbed—e.g. horror—or if I feel nothing at all, then I tend not to like it. If it causes me think and run through the gamut of emotions, then I tend to love them. If I find that a certain character resonates with me, I then love that movie, and that is precisely why *Soldier* ranks high on my list of favorites: I completely relate with the main character, Todd, and the character growth he experiences throughout this movie.

I feel that *Soldier* is something far deeper than a late-90s action flick. The following analysis is based on my personal insights of this film. If the creators of the movie intended any of the material to actually be interpreted in this manner, then my hat is off to them for doing so. That said, I understand that any piece of art can be picked to death during attempts to determine what the artist "really meant" when they created it. Again, my intent here is to explain the portions of the film that, for me, have great significance. Let me assign an overall theme to this movie, and then I will lead you down the garden path and show you all the nuances that led me to this conclusion. There are other themes in this movie that I will briefly touch upon, but the primary one I want to examine is this: *Soldier* is about coming to terms with one's own past. Don't believe me? Well, follow along and see how you feel by the end of this analysis. Allow me to assume that you've seen *Soldier* and are familiar with the conditioning that our protagonist, Todd 3465, has gone through. Todd was possibly bred or outright stolen to be raised from birth in the "Adam Project." Adam Project boys were indoctrinated with constant audio propaganda and with visual and physical violence. It's made apparent that Todd is the strongest and smartest of all of the boys. He excels at every test and is the perfect model of non-emotion. (I'll surmise here that the entire "training" sequence portrayed in the film could be a commentary on how we raise and educate children in modern societies. Not that we are excessively harsh with children, but we do "program" them to become workforce fodder. We teach them from young ages that what you "do" is all that you are.) Todd's non-emotion and willingness to follow orders without question is made especially clear during the target-practice session when Todd shoots through the "innocent" dummy in order to kill the "enemy." Perhaps another commentary on results being what matter, not how you achieve them.

When Todd graduates from the Adam Project at the age of seventeen, he is given his rank, insignia, and his number, 3465. From that moment on, he is nothing more and nothing less than a soldier. Twenty-three years pass and all the while Todd and his fellow soldiers dutifully carry out every order that is given to them. And all the while, time is passing and the soldiers are, indeed, getting older and getting closer and closer to their "retirement"—perhaps not so different from replicants. And the soldiers getting older becomes the crux of the matter. There is a new, younger, stronger, faster, more enhanced batch of soldiers being pitted against the original Adam Project group. They compete in various exercises and Todd 3465 is up against Caine 607 in a 15-mile run which, of course, Todd loses. And all of this leads us to the climactic aerial battle "up the chains" that is the end of Todd the soldier as he plummets 30 or 40 feet to the ground and "dies," thus opening the door for Todd the human being to finally enter the world.

Soldier manages to compress all of this important backstory and exposition into its opening sixteen minutes; an impressive feat that never fails to draw me in and prepare me for the beginning of Todd's personal Hero's Journey. As mentioned, Todd did certainly "die" when he hit the ground. The old Todd is dead, and a new Todd "awakens" to the reality of life on the garbage planet, Arcadia 234. Todd is dumped out of the space-going garbage scow and onto a completely foreign environment. He is the "stranger in a strange land" at this point. He is confused and hurting and he gets more and more injured by the weather and landscape in this strange new place.

He eventually stumbles his way into a settlement—the home of the passengers of a colony ship that flew off course and crashed 12 years earlier—but the environment raises its ugly fist again and sends him crashing down some stairs and into their lives. The people know that Todd is a soldier and they are afraid of him, but they also feel that accepting him and taking care of him while he is injured is the "right thing to do." Enter Sandra. Here is the first soft, caring person that Todd has ever had in his life. Some people may look at this movie and think his glances and interactions with her are sexual in nature, but this is absolutely not the case—except, perhaps, in some Freudian manner. The truth of the matter is that Sandra is the Mother archetype, and the only mother-type that Todd has ever had. She talks to Todd gently and treats him gently. She teaches him the very basics of survival on Arcadia: from planting vegetables to cooking meals. Todd also learns from her that one can be soft as well as strong when he sees Sandra kill one of the venomous serpents in the garden. She does so quickly and efficiently, and it should be noted here that the serpents in the film are a very clear metaphor for fear and danger.

Sandra's husband, Mace, also acts as one of Todd's teachers, but his role is more understated and he is not a Father to Todd, but Mace could be termed as an appropriate authority figure—a replacement of sorts for Todd's harsh military commanders. Sandra and Mace have one son, Nathan, and Nathan's role is extremely poetic and important in this movie even though he never says a word. He cannot speak due to a long illness caused by a bite from one of the venomous serpents. However, the role of Nathan here is not to play the son, but to represent Todd's repressed inner child and Todd's stolen innocence.

Todd's rising consciousness is expressed in the time-passing montage that takes place about thirty minutes into the film. When I think about it, it's an odd scene to have in what is considered to be an action film, but it works, because, as I've mentioned, this actually is a drama. Drama that is most powerfully demonstrated when Todd is cutting carrots for dinner and he slices his finger with the knife. After minimal pause, he just keeps cutting away—no reaction to the cut, the pain, or the blood. Sandra sees this and takes Todd's hand. This is significant because it's quite possibly the first time he has ever been touched with any kind of tenderness. She bandages his wound and then she asks him what it is like to be a soldier. She asks him what he thinks about. She asks him what he feels. No one has ever asked him these questions before. No one has ever been kind to him. No one has ever bandaged his wounds in care for him as a person. Being patched up after battles was likely more akin to vehicle repair and maintenance rather than any kind of healing act. This is all new to him, and for a brief moment, he glances over at Nathan who is sitting and playing in the background. This moment is the inner child being given a voice and being allowed to speak for the first time about what he feels: "Fear," he answers her. "Fear?" Sandra questions. "Fear and discipline," he responds. "Now?" Sandra is shocked. "Always," says Todd.

Sandra is so appalled by this answer that she tries to hug Todd, assuming to bring him some sense of comfort. Todd, though, has never been hugged before. It actually increases his fear to the point that he starts to shake—most likely in an effort not to flee the situation. Sandra releases the hug when she realizes he is uncomfortable with that amount of closeness. It's extremely difficult to know how to react to a situation when your senses are always overwhelmed and on high-alert.

Which brings us to the Christmas party scene—a scene I particularly love because I understand exactly how Todd is feeling in this situation. Todd sees Sandra and Mace and Nathan sharing the tender moment of opening gifts, he sees people laughing and dancing and having fun. The party is loud and raucous and, for Todd, it really is overwhelming. There is too much input, and the noise starts giving him PTSD-type flashbacks. Todd disappears from the party. He cannot reconcile this new life he has with his old life. He cannot understand how he could have been the killing soldier and now he is surrounded by friends and loving people. And this is the part of the scene that I love so much: we see Todd watching the party through a skylight on the roof. He still wants to participate, but he needs to do it from a distance so it doesn't overwhelm him. He watches the revelry for a while, and then he sits back to think and reflect on everything that he is experiencing and feeling. And the next day reveals the result of Todd's ruminating. He has set up a steel fuel-tank as a punching bag, and he is tearing into it. Sandra tells others that he is "exercising," but I think the better word here is "exorcising"—as in casting out demons. For the first time in his life, Todd is angry. As he punches the steel, memories of his life flash through his mind. How he was treated as a child. What he was forced to hear, what he was forced to do, how he was forced to be. And then he is flashing back to battles and things he did simply because he was ordered to do so. He is probably realizing at this point that nobody forced him to do anything, it just seemed that way. So, his anger is focused on the people who made him what he was and on himself for not being different and choosing a better path. Again, this is another scene where I really empathize with Todd. I've gone through very similar emotional battles, so I love seeing this internal struggle given this external imagery.

Todd then does what so many of us do when we are absorbed in our misery and when we are angry: he accidentally lashes out at someone he cares about. He nearly kills one of the only friends he has ever had; someone who really looks up to him. Todd realizes his mistake just in time and releases his friend, but the damage is done and the settlement members begin to question whether Todd is capable of living among them for much longer. The scene of Todd beating the fuel tank continues, but now Todd is exhausted. His hands are bloodied, the rags he was using for gloves are shredded. He is wore out and tired of fighting. Pay attention to where he drops his hands because it is so noteworthy. Todd surrenders and lets go of his anger. He realizes that his anger is only hurting himself and others close to him now. He realizes that nothing more can be done about the situation. That was then, and this is the here and now.

Okay, let's move onto the next scene, and I'm going to describe this scene in a little more detail and then back it up to explain what I'm seeing. There is a lot going on in this scene within a short span of time, and it's also a really strong moment between Todd and Nathan. Nathan shows Todd that he has solved a puzzle game that he has been working on. As Nathan turns around to leave, he sees that one of the green, venomous snakes is in the room. As mentioned before, Nathan was almost killed by one of these creatures and he is extremely afraid of them. Todd reacts instantly, but not in the way you might expect. He throws a heavy boot to Nathan and motions for the child to pick it up. Nathan doesn't move. Todd then pantomimes clobbering the snake with the boot. Nathan still doesn't move. Todd smacks the boot on the bed again, but the snake strikes out at Nathan, and Todd must save the boy. He catches the snake in mid-air, stares it in the face, and then Todd tosses the snake back in the corner and nods to Nathan to go and kill it with the boot.

Unfortunately, Sandra and Mace only see this last part happen. Mace kills the snake and demands to know what Todd was doing. Todd, of course, makes no response. His training and conditioning really do not allow for him to speak up for himself—especially to someone in authority. Okay, let's back this scene up and go through the important images and remember, as I have already pointed out, Nathan represents Todd's inner child: the child who never got to be. So, let's look at the puzzle game—this is significant imagery of Todd unlocking another emotional puzzle within himself. Is it related to the dream Todd had just awoke from? Is Todd saying to himself, "Ah, that's why I'm the way I am"? Also remember that Todd said that he always feels afraid when he voiced how the child inside him feels. When Todd tosses the boot to Nathan, he is saying, "You don't have to be afraid anymore. Don't worry, I am here with you. We are in this together. Kill the snake. Kill your fear."

And look at this moment of Todd catching the snake: he stares it in the face... Todd is facing his fear and proving to his inner child that they don't have to be afraid of this thing. They can face it together. Still, the inner child does not understand all this quite yet. He has not yet embraced the idea that he is now this big, powerful man. To him, the world is still a big, scary place. Unfortunately, with Mace and Sandra now angry with him, Todd has no one to speak for him at the village council, and he is asked to leave the settlement. This provides us with yet another significant scene before this drama film actually becomes the action movie it was purported to be. As Todd sits in a sheltered area, alone and lonely and most likely believing that he is incapable of living any type of "normal" life, he begins to cry. He is actually confused by the tears and touches his face to figure out what this water is. The beautiful moment is this: he doesn't try to stop crying. Todd lets the tears flow and actually feels his grief and pain. It is so important to understand that when Todd has emotional reactions, that he does not judge them nor try to stop them from happening. Every time it happens, he just feels the emotion and works through it. It's a lesson we all need to learn and practice. Feel your emotions. Embrace them. Understand them. Don't push them down where they fester and become future, toxic problems.

Back at the settlement, Nathan rescues his parents from one of the serpents by pulling it off their bed and killing it with a heavy boot. Sandra and Mace realize that Todd had been trying to teach their son an important lesson, not trying to harm him. Mace runs out to invite Todd back to stay. However, when Mace finds Todd and apologizes, it happens as a patrol ship carrying the new batch of soldiers lands on Arcadia. The truth is always out there and our past will always come back to haunt us until we truly atone for it and make peace with it. Todd knows that this arrival is an ominous event. The soldiers are not there to rescue the people, they are merely there for training exercises and they will exterminate anyone in their path. This is an interesting point in Todd's new life as this is the first time that he knows what is going on and no one else does, thus we get a bit of a shift in his demeanor.

Todd and Mace begin running back to the settlement, but the two men are fired upon. Mace is mortally wounded and, as he dies, he begs Todd to protect Sandra and Nathan. Todd promises in his usual silent manner, but the look on his face says it all: the soldiers have killed his friend, now it's personal. We see a different Todd here as he kills the first three soldiers that have entered the settlement. He is in his element. He is in command. No one else can do what needs to be done. He is efficient and ruthless. He is exactly what his puppet-masters made him to be, but they no longer control him. Thinking they are up against a significant amount of resistance, the rest of the soldiers withdraw in order to make their counter-attack under cover of darkness.

Most of the fighting and killing sequences are only here to make this the action movie it is supposed to be, but before that begins we get one more scene between Todd and Sandra and Nathan. Todd is getting ready to fight the rest of the unit and Nathan finds Todd stockpiling and loading weapons taken off of the dead soldiers. This is the inner child, without fear, seeing the grown soldier, also without fear, for the first time. The inner child accepts that this is necessary and that this is what he has become. This is the moment he was trained for. This is the time when all of that pain and suffering can be put to use to fight for something he truly believes in. He hasn't been ordered to go and do this. He is doing it because he wants to. Because it is the right thing to do. Because he is the only one who can do something about it. (A side-note here: as I went through and edited this script for publication, I realized that my YouTube channel has become a moment that I've trained my whole life for. I keep learning amazing lessons from this "crap movie." Side-note done. On we go.) As the scene continues Sandra and Todd have a conversation that could be construed as the man leaving the care of his mother. He claims he has to do this on his own, she cannot coddle him any longer.

Then, as Todd puts on a few streaks of camouflage, we see the soldier fully formed. He has fully integrated his new life with his old life. It does not mean that he is a soldier forever and that is all he will ever be. It means that he is a soldier right now because that is what he needs to be right now. I must admit that I do love the line Todd speaks here. I mean, who doesn't? "I'm going to kill them all, sir." The fighting commences, and I won't bother running through any of the exposition to cover that. Suffice it to say that Todd triumphs over the other soldiers and there is, of course, one final, epic battle between Todd and his nemesis, Caine 607. I suppose this fight could be viewed as a battle between the Old Todd or Shadow Todd and the New Todd—battling one's self is such a common trope and psychological thread to pull. However, let's take a step back and shift our perspective of this fight: What I see as Todd prevails over Caine is a moment of compassion and mourning. Todd wraps Caine in a headlock and, as Caine expresses fear for the first time, Todd expresses sorrow and mourns for Caine's sad existence and the necessity of killing him. He breaks Caine's neck and then lowers him gently to the ground as if he were his closest friend and not his mortal enemy.

With the enemy vanquished, Todd and the villagers and the rest of the old batch of soldiers take over the patrol ship, kick out what is left of the bad guys (two of Todd's previous commanding officers and a smarmy colonel—god, I love Jason Isaacs), and they head for space and the Trinity Moons—the place the villagers were headed 12 years earlier. A typical, happy, Hollywood ending. At this time, I won't go into the entire metaphor of leaving the planet of garbage where we struggle and wallow and sailing to paradise. I'm saving that for a future analysis. But we aren't quite done with *Soldier* yet.

It still has one final, dramatic scene to offer: Nathan makes his way to the bridge of the ship to find Todd. When he gets there, he raises his arms up in the gesture of asking Todd to pick him up. Here is the inner child finally ready to embrace the Man. Todd picks Nathan up and the two of them look out a window upon the stars. Todd has come to terms with his past. The man and the inner child are now at peace; each fully accepting who and what they were and who and what they have become. What we see happening in Todd's life throughout this movie is a drastic change in character and personal understanding that can happen to anyone who has an experience that awakens their sleeping consciousness. The person is living their "normal existence," they have an awakening experience—which tends to be traumatic in nature—and they become something new and different from what they once were. *Soldier* is the classic Hero's Journey mythology in every sense, but I believe that the creators of this movie went above and beyond in their attempts to display Todd's awakening consciousness. Whether that was their intent or if it was something from deep within the human subconscious, it was beautifully executed. This is a story we see over and over again, and we need to keep seeing it because the majority of people seeing it are still not comprehending it.

Todd is the Hero archetype who takes the left-hand path and becomes something different than what he was before. He didn't ask to take this journey—one rarely chooses the difficult road—and he didn't know where it was going to lead, but he clearly wound up in a better place in spite of all the pain and suffering he experienced. That's what pain and suffering are for: to bring you to a better place...if you let them.

And there we have it. My interpretation of the spiritual and deeply emotional elements I see within the movie *Soldier* and, thus, why I love this movie.

Cult-Movie Review: Soldier

by John Kenneth Muir

Soldier (1998), starring Kurt Russell, is a space-age variation on the same tale, but without many of the philosophical contradictions that made the Stallone film such a challenging and vital work of art.

In *First Blood*, Rambo launched a one man war against a civilian town in the Pacific Northwest, and so the lines between good guy and bad guy were blurred. In *Soldier*, Russell's character, Todd, defends a village of defenseless citizens from rampaging, genetically-engineered soldiers who have rendered him and his kind "obsolete." Thus, Todd must never traverse what we could consider difficult ethical or moral boundaries. On the contrary, Todd proves his mettle to the civilians in battle, which was the very thing that Rambo ultimately found impossible to do.

Soldier was directed by Paul Anderson, who in 1997 gave the world a very effective space-horror film, *Event Horizon*. Yet *Soldier* feels like a step down from that movie, both in terms of complexity and visualization. There's a kind of claustrophobia or sound-stage-like feel to *Soldier*'s exterior scenes, and much footage is recycled (particularly in a musical montage), or slowed down to make it seem more effectively shot...as though not enough good material was captured during production.

Despite the stage-y feel and botched editing of *Soldier*, the film boasts a remarkable strength that goes a long way towards repairing the aspects of the drama that don't work. That strength is named Kurt Russell. Again and again Anderson focuses intently on Russell's soulful, haunted eyes—frequently in extreme close-up—and so a powerful connection is forged between the character, Todd, and the audience. Throughout the film we see Todd involved in horrible violence, and wonder if that means he is an unfeeling monster. Russell's eyes tell us that he is not.

Russell has very few lines of dialogue in *Soldier*, and yet he is a powerful central presence, and an emotional one. Russell never gets a "raw" monologue like Stallone's in *First Blood*—an emotional catharsis that explodes off the screen—but instead he carries that sad, tortured countenance throughout the narrative, and this approach is, broadly-speaking, effective.

Intriguingly, Todd's predicament is not that he doesn't fit in. It's that he has never known how to live because he has never been anything other than a soldier. Todd doesn't know what it means to truly be with other people, to be near children or women. But he has good instincts (and a good heart…) and the film suggests that these elements of his emotional gestalt represent the starting point of his journey to join, at long last, the human race.

That's a powerful notion, and occasionally *Soldier* alights on a strong image to go with it, like soldiers being dumped, literally, in the trash, unwanted by society, amid the flotsam and jetsam of the military-industrial complex, which produces new war machines—and soldiers—at a prodigious rate.

Reviews for *Soldier* were quite savage in 1998, mostly for the flaws I note above, yet director Anderson undeniably makes the most out of Russell's screen presence, so much that that *Soldier* proves unexpectedly powerful in spots, and an intriguing if compromised effort to bring the *First Blood* aesthetic to the final frontier.

"Soldiers deserve soldiers"

In 1996, the Adam Project is initiated. It is a rigorous military training program in which babies are taken and trained by the Army from birth. The children are exposed to bloody violence at a young age, and then encouraged to show strength—and no mercy—even to one another. They study tactics and train to be physically superior.

The greatest of the Adam Project soldiers is Todd (Russell), a soldier who fights multiple successful campaigns, including the War of the Six Cities, the Moscow Incident, and the War of the Argentine Moons.

After decades in service, however, under sympathetic Captain Church (Gary Busey), Todd and his comrades are rendered obsolete by a new generation of genetically-engineered soldiers.

When Colonel Mekum's (Jason Isaac) new soldiers, led by Caine (Jason Scott Lee), defeat Todd and two others in a training exercise, Todd is left for dead and transported to Arcadia 234, a disposal planet far out in space. Alone and without a war to fight, Todd explores the inhospitable planet until he finds a small colony of crash survivors, who have been living on Arcadia in peace for twelve years. A family, consisting of Mace, Sandra, and little

Nathan, nurse Todd back to health. The colonists are wary of Todd because all he can do is wage war, and at one point, resolve to send him away, fearing he represents a threat to their continued survival.

Before long, however, Colonel Mekum, Caine, and the new soldiers arrive on the planet for a training exercise and immediately classify the colony as hostile. Now Todd has a new war to fight, with the future of his friends at stake.

"FEAR AND DISCIPLINE...ALWAYS"

Soldier borrows from *First Blood* (1982) and other 1980s action films, such as *Missing in Action* (1984), and thus qualifies as a futuristic pastiche. For instance, Gary Busey plays likable if stern Captain Church, a surrogate for Richard Crenna's character, Trautman, in the *Rambo* saga. In both cases, a sympathetic military officer—sometimes aligned with a hostile military or law enforcement hierarchy—offers common-sense counsel about his preferred soldier (John Rambo/Todd), but is routinely ignored. When the military hierarchy, here represented by Mekum, fails to defeat that soldier, Trautman/Church is there to warn that the renegade and "real" soldier has been underestimated, and that his "war" is righteous.

Similarly, *Soldier* re-stages action moments we've seen in a lot of these war films. At one point, Todd hides in a river from the enemy soldiers, and rises up, with a machine gun, from the placid water, to open fire on them. We've seen this shot in many, many films, but I remember it specifically from Chuck Norris's *Missing in Action.* Similarly, some folks may see the idea of a soldier without a nation defending a harmless colony as evoking *Seven Samurai* (1954) or *The Magnificent Seven* (1960), as well.

But *Soldier* seems half-formed, or half-conceived, in the sense that it never takes a stance on the fact the opening scenes of the film reveal Todd as a cold-blooded killer (for his country). We see him in action, doing much the same horrible things that Caine does later, on Arcadia. Specifically, we see him murdering unarmed civilians. The idea may be that by being cast-out and ignored by those he once served, Todd gains his humanity, but again, Todd never really grapples explicitly with that concept. He never seems to doubt who he is or why he was made, and instead merely uses his skills to kill the soldiers who threaten the colony.

Yet—significantly—the new soldiers like Caine are serving very much as Todd once served: without question. There is only a hint of Todd's awareness of this fact when he notes that "soldiers deserve soldiers," an acknowledgement of an unspoken brotherhood, even with the enemy. Even bad soldiers deserve to die, apparently, at the hands of other soldiers.

Oppositely, however, *Soldier* often does a fine job of explaining Todd's mind-set as a soldier. "Fear and discipline...always," he states.

Those qualities represent the impetus that drives him to fight and kill for a cause that isn't truly his. By contrast, Todd's defense of the colony—protection of the innocent—seems to be the thing that spurs his re-birth as a human being. He fights on this occasion not out of fear or discipline, but out of a desire to protect those that he has come to care about. He has learned that civilians aren't merely human shields, but it would be great if we saw how Todd came to that reckoning in more persuasive and explicit terms.

Although some of *Soldier's* visuals now seem dated because of the CGI, the alien planet still looks terrific in long shot. The piles of of trash reaching to the Heavens seem to forecast the post-apocalyptic Earth of *Wall-E* (2008), and the nature of the "cast-off" garbage is important too.

We see the Liberty Bell in the garbage heap on the disposal ship, for instance, a suggestion that in this future, freedom and liberty are dead. Similarly, we see a giant aircraft carrier dumped on its side, left there on the surface. It is an avatar for military waste and the grinding gears of so-called technological "progress." A new machine replaces an old machine, just as a new soldier replaces an old soldier. Such visuals suggest that the human race is very good and dreaming new, more efficient ways, to kill and destroy

Alas, the scenes involving actors on the ground (and not CGI landscapes) look very stage-bound, and somewhat cheap. We see again and again the same terrain, where a large steel machine (looking a bit like the up-turned rib cage of a giant dinosaur) stands. Even with vehicles and men moving back and forth, the battle scenes seem very limited in terms of scope and grandeur. This is also true in the opening montage, where we see Todd go on numerous missions throughout his career. The war zones look very obviously like stage sets, and there is something rudimentary, even slap-dash about the staging, as small groups of soldiers march left-to-right across a short zone, guns blazing.

One more step, and they would walk off the set...

Soldier is also scuttled, to some degree, by the cartoon nature of Colonel Mekum's villainy. He demonstrates such consistent bad judgment and such cowardice that one wonders how he ever ascended to his position of authority. At every chance, Mekum makes the wrong, mean, dumb decision, and then his character is completely undercut by the moment in which Todd grabs him and he pisses his pants. Instead of being presented as a clever, dangerous opponent, Mekum is a straw man who is easily brought down so that Todd looks stronger, smarter, and better than those he opposes. Like Teasle in *First Blood*, there is no overt or clear-cut motivation for Mekum's cruelty. He's an arrogant jerk, it seems, simply to move the story along from one point to the next.

All these aspects of *Soldier* diminish the film, and yet, on the other hand, you've got Russell. Although I grew up in the eighties with Arnold Schwarzenegger, Stallone, Norris, Seagal, Van Damme, and other "action heroes," Russell has always been my favorite. As Snake Plissken, Jack Burton, R.J. MacReady, and Gabriel Cash, Russell projects more than mere physical strength—he projects cunning, humanity, bemusement, and, finally, a sense that he is a real human being, not a super-man impervious to bullets.

Because he is an actor first, an action hero second, Russell is always able to excavate and convey hidden layers of a character's psyche, and that's precisely what he does here. His Todd thus comes across as both a great soldier and an innocent in terms of human emotions. He is both incredibly strong and incredibly vulnerable.

We see that despite Todd's strength and power, he is, essentially, a child. His emotional development is arrested. He knows nothing of what it means to be human, and his attempts to be human are awkward and not always successful. Similarly, when he fails in his endeavors, Todd resorts to might—a punching bag that bloodies his knuckles, because that is all he has ever known: resolution through violence.

Anderson proves adroit in his use of Russell in the film, both in terms of the near ubiquitous close-ups (which showcase Russell's gentle eyes) and his placement in the frame. There are several times, for instance, in the film, where Todd is blocked in the action as being apart or separated from the rest of the colonists. At one point, he is framed through a window, cursed to be the outsider, and never a participant. Later, he sits alone, outside the colony buildings, and is bracketed by machines that have been re-purposed from junk by the colonists. The implication is that he too is trying to re-purpose himself to be useful in his new environments.

Another nicely-lensed sequence that showcases the essence of Russell's sensitivity in this role involves his quiet yearning for Sandra (Connie Nielson). As she speaks to him, folding laundry, Todd's gaze wanders. We see slow, detailed shots of her eyes, her mouth, even her chest, and we realize this is Todd's point of view. This may sound lascivious, but it doesn't play that way. Instead, it plays out as an extended, almost sensual moment… because Todd is innocent, feeling the first longings of desire. It's not rude (as it sounds…), just his first attempts at "exploring" (with his eyes) the beauty of a woman, an aspect of humanity he hasn't known.

As a pastiche of war movies like *First Blood, Soldier* resurrects a lot of clichés, but for the space age. I noted so above, but the movie has a lot of running from explosions, decoys that fool the bad guys, and other familiar set-pieces. The staging and execution of a lot of the action leaves something to be desired and yet I have returned to watch *Soldier* (1998) probably three or four times since I saw it in the late 1990s. For all its flaws, the movie does manage to make us care about Todd and mourn the fact that he was taken from his family and made to be a killer. We understand that he could be so much more.

How could *Soldier* have been better? Well, I concur with Church's words to Mekum. Director Paul Anderson should have made the movie "smarter" instead of "fast." The power of Russell's strong but vulnerable performance drags *Soldier* over the finish line with a surprising amount of success, but with a little more back-up from the director and screenwriter in terms of execution and originality the movie—like the film's hero—could have transcended expectations for it.

"Your Men are obsolete": The critical reception

Soldier was shot from January until May 1998 in Burbank, California, on the Warner Brothers stages 12, 16, 19, 20 and a gravel pit in Azusa. Soldier was, at the time, one of the most expensive movies ever made to go direct to video in the UK. It reportedly had a budget in the range of $60 to 75 million. Warner Brothers released *Soldier* and *Blade Runner*, and the films have many things in common, including being the same screenwriter. Both were box-office failures and had a mixed critical reception but have gained a cult following. The critical reception for *Soldier* was unforgivingly hostile. To begin with, this review from [18]*San Francisco Examiner* critic Bob Stevens: "The celluloid equivalent of the junkyard planet on which this piece of garbage is appropriately set."

I think this best describes what happened to the film in a sense is what happened to the main character. It was metaphorical of the film, and over time I believe that people who haven't seen it or noticed it before can appreciate it a lot more.

"It's a big, clanging, brutal, actioner in which we search the murk in vain for the sparks of humanity the moviemakers keep promising us," declared [19]Michael Wilmington of *The Chicago Tribune*. "*Soldier* wants to be an intense thriller with cerebral significance, but suffers from self-seriousness and silly cliches," agreed [20]Christine James of *Boxoffice Magazine*.

Soldier has much significance in our world, and we need only consider the indoctrination that has been at play. The critics above stated *Soldier* as clanging, brutal, and wanting to have cerebral significance. There's no doubt

[18] *San Francisco Examiner critic Bob Stevens (October 23, 1998)*

[19] *Michael Wilmington of The Chicago Tribune (October 23, 1998)*

[20] *Christine James of Boxoffice Magazine (June 5, 2002)*

that it's brutal, but it still brings something of quality to the table with its variety of themes at play that involves warfare and power politics between the characters of Church and Colonel Mekum, what it means to be human with Todd 3465, ageism, identity, and the advancement of technology with Caine 607.

While the [21]*Daily News* from New York called the film a dang *Shane*, they mention the influence of the past genre as stated. It's no secret that the Western was once America's most popular and most representative genre and has gone undercover as the science fiction film. When *Star Wars* came out in 1977, many critics noted its similarity to John Ford's 1956 classic *The Searchers*. And 1981's *Outland* was an acknowledged remake of *High Noon*, with Sean Connery's space marshal standing in for Gary Cooper. *Soldier* is a sci-fi rewrite of *Shane*, with a screenplay by David Webb Peoples, the author of *Blade Runner* and *Unforgiven*.

The more positive reviews understood its intentions. "It resonates on more levels than just a simple action film," asserted [22]Robert Roten of *Laramie Movie Scope*. "*Soldier* is a compact sci-fi Western about a gunslinging super-soldier who must protect a small community from his former comrades. Like the '50s cowboy and cavalry flicks to which it is indebted, the movie is compulsively unpretentious; nothing here suggests that the filmmakers had any goal in mind except to tell a self-contained genre story with maximum efficiency," wrote [23]*AV Club* reviewer Ignatiy Vishnevetsky. "This appealing formulaic action adventure displays a lot of conviction in its not-too-flashy action scenes and a little levity in the gradual socialization of Russell's character," asserted the [24]*Chicago Reader's* Lisa Alspector.

[25]Pvt.Caboose91 of *manlymovie.net* said, "To the credit of Peoples and Anderson, *Soldier* takes its time to build the characters and observe Todd as he struggles to ingratiate himself into a more peaceful culture. Peoples' script has a number of things on its mind, exploring if it's possible for a lifelong killing machine to assimilate themselves back into society." [26]Los Angeles Times writer Kevin Thomas called the film "a potent comic-book-style action-adventure." "Russell is quite suitable for a Terminator-like role, where dialogue is at an absolute minimum, physical intimidation is relevant,

[21] *Critic David Kehr of Daily News from New York (October 23, 1998)*
[22] *Robert Roten of Laramie Movie Scope (October 24, 1998)*
[23] *AV Club reviewer Ignatiy Vishnevetsky (May 28, 2013)*
[24] *Chicago Reader's Lisa Alspector (October 26, 1998)*
[25] *Pvt.Caboose91 manlymovie.net (March 8, 2015)*
[26] *Los Angeles Times writer Kevin Thomas (October 23, 1998)*

and action sequences are numerous," explained [27]Mike Massie of *Gone With the Twins.*

> "The movie features a wildly underrated performance by Kurt Russell, a highly imaginative production design, a large amount of brutal and bloody violence, a salient social statement on militaristic brainwash, a cool *Blade Runner* connection, and perhaps most fun of all, some pretty kickass action blows that cut deep and leave a mark!" [28]—Jake Dee, www.joblo.com

"Kudos to David Tattersall's photography and David L. Snyder's production design. The training headquarters and spaceship are sleek, while the planet is a depressing, claustrophobic heap of junk and swirling storms. A supporting cast is allowed some glints of personality: Gary Busey is Todd's former captain and Jason Isaacs is the sadistic Colonel Mekum, who decides the planet is expendable. And one elegiac nod to the past is sounded in this movie about the awful future: Joel McNelly's musical score steals the trumpet solo from *Patton*; it's a haunting note. (from the [29]*Clarion-Ledger* from Jackson, Mississippi) ·

"As written by David Webb Peoples (the former Connecticut boy behind *Blade Runner* and *Unforgiven*) and directed by Paul Anderson, *Soldier* charges forward as a heavily visual, frequently violent saga of future shock. This is an often brutal war movie, devoid of light and jocularity—though not of lust and sentiment. Those in search of a good-time dating picture should not land here. Yet, like Russell, Anderson's film exerts a certain muscular pull." (from the [30]*Hartford Courant* from Hartford, Connecticut)

Soldier may not have struck a chord with critics or audiences at the time of its release, but I hope it influences and finds new admirers today. To end this film's reception, I have to quote Colonel Mekum as he states in *Soldier*, "The mind controls the body, after all. And we're doing such wonderful things with the mind." I hope that reading this book educates and gives an understanding of the Western genre, opens up whole new interpretations of the film *Soldier*, and gets people thinking cerebrally even in its simplicity. The finest stories are often the simplest.

---

[27] *Mike Massie of Gone With the Twins https://gonewiththetwins.com/new/soldier-1998/soldier/*

[28] *The F*cking Black Sheep: Soldier (1998) By Jake Dee (July 19, 2019) https://www.joblo.com/the-fcking-black-sheep-soldier-1998/*

[29] *Clarion-Ledger from Jackson, Mississippi · Page 46 (October 22, 1998)*

[30] *Malcom Jonson; Courant Film Critic. Hartford Courant (October 22, 1998)*

Afterword: Other's Obsessions

by Paul M. Sammon

We all have them.

Well…let's amend that first sentence.

Some of us have them.

Obsessions.

Not passions, mind you. Those emotions, inflamed as they may be, sit one rung below the all-consuming fixations we *obsessionally* assign to life- altering people, places, things. Transformational encounters that pierce our defenses to relentlessly grip our hearts.

The spectrum spanning such preoccupations can be vast. Refusing to let go of the disastrous youthful rupture of our first broken heart. Retaining a rabid belief in the salvational aspects of traditional religions. Subscribing to the dreadful certainty that we suffer under the baleful gaze of a fallen angel, who views our never-ending human follies through hate-filled, world- controlling eyes.

Or perhaps we simply, lovingly revisit the unexpected suffusion of joy we sensed upon viewing a particular piece of art. An impactful film, let's say. Which resulted in the literal physical epiphany of suddenly feeling the hair follicles on your arm standing straight up, while pulling bumps of skin along with them. A phenomenon the medical community terms horripila-tion, piloerection, or cutis anserina. Goose bumps.

Danny Stewart has felt horripilation. He also understands the proclivity towards obsession and the equal urge to share. The evidence resides in this book, Danny's book, which he has spent so much effort and love to bring to your attention.

Danny's obsession with the 1998 film *Soldier* is evident throughout, particularly in the wide-ranging information he has uncovered, underscored by how he's *not* employed the currently fashionable, despicably lax practice of simply collating and/or citing previously published material to manufacture a manuscript falsely claimed as one's own. No, Danny has gone to the source(s), speaking to and deep-diving with *Soldier's* cast and crew to profile the history of a particular recruit he so obviously cares for.

I applaud Danny's effort and empathize with his obsession. My own passions involve movies, music, photography and books. I have, in turn, written a few of the latter. The best known being *Future Noir: The Making of Blade Runner*.

Interestingly, the original introduction to the first, 1996 edition of *Future Noir* was titled "One Man's Obsession." That intro detailed mine own ongoing fascination with Ridley Scott's 1982 groundbreaker. So how could I not ping to the fact, while originally viewing *Soldier* back in 1998, that its scenarist was David Webb Peoples and its Production designer David L. Snyder, two men who'd respectively served as *Blade Runner's* co-screenwriter and Art Director? Or how could I possibly miss *Soldier's* evocative inclusion of a junked BR "Spinner" or its references to BR's Tannhauser Gate?

David Peoples' subsequent statement that *Soldier* might be considered a shared universe "sidequel" to Blade Runner (or that its BR bits were an in- joke generated during production) did elevate my opinion of director Paul W.S. Anderson's own film. But not by much. While I do appreciate the obsessional archaeology Danny has brought to his *Soldier* book, the film's overriding defects, in my estimation, remain the same; Peoples' potentially intriguing crypto-Western screenplay, with its subtextual questioning of dehumanizing lock-step military mindsets, was undone by pedestrian direction, misjudged horror flourishes, and a listless pace.

No matter. This is Danny's book, not mine. His passion, not my own. And I respect his devotion towards a certain metaphorical leaf which may not result in my cup of tea. So brew away, my friend.

A final thought.

Despite my disregard for *Soldier* I – weirdly – uncovered a more intimate linkage between this film and yet another. Unexpectedly discovered while doing some cinematic snooping of my own.

In order to best to compose this piece I started researching. Eventually I stumbled upon an online, then-contemporary *Soldier* trailer. Only to be smacked in the brain by an image with far greater personal resonance than anything coupling *Soldier* to BR.

That *Soldier* trailer begins with medium closeup of a weightless astronaut drifting in space. The camera tracks along the rocketeers's spacesuit before stopping at a closeup of its helmet. Whose open, battered, shattered visor cradles a shriveled skeletal face.

This shot startled me in a manner only I could understand. For it immediately brought me back to my first cinematic trauma, at the age of four, when, in a crowded Japanese theater, I witnessed an eerily similar shot near the climax of producer Ivan Tors low-fi science fiction fantasy *Rider to the Stars* – a shock cut to a dead drifting astronaut, from whose smashed face-plate grimaced nearly the same desiccated, eyeless face. My unformed mind had been horrified by this grisly visage. So much so that I'd run screaming and crying from the the theater, rocked to my core.

That single skull-in-a-helmet image still haunts. Obsessionally, if you will. How strange, then, and how strangely fitting, to discover, nearly seven decades after my initial searing fright, that such a close visual cousin lurked within a throwaway *Soldier* promo.

I suppose this means I've found something else to obsess about. Thanks, Danny.

—Central Florida August 2022

Film Credits

Director
Paul W.S. Anderson (as Paul Anderson)

Writer
David Webb Peoples

Produced by

Jeremy Bolt	...	co-producer
Susan Ekins	...	executive producer
Fred Fontana	...	associate producer
R.J. Louis	...	executive producer
James G. Robinson	...	executive producer
Jerry Weintraub	...	producer

Music by
Joel McNeely

Cinematography by

David Tattersall	...	director of photography
Oliver Wood	...	director of photography: added scenes

Film Editing by
Martin Hunter

Casting By
Mindy Marin

Production Design by
David L. Snyder

Art Direction by

Thomas Valentine	...	(as Tom Valentine)
Paul Sonski	...	Assistant Art Director

Set Decoration by

Kate Sullivan	...	(as Kate J. Sullivan)

Costume Design by
Erica Edell Phillips

Makeup Department

Janis Clark	...	hair stylist
Carolyn Elias	...	hair stylist
Greg LaCava	...	makeup artist
Mark Landon	...	makeup artist
Steve LaPorte	...	key makeup artist / makeup effects artist (as Steve Laporte)
Dennis Liddiard	...	makeup artist: Mr. Russell (as G. Dennis Liddiard)
Peter Montagna	...	makeup artist
Peggy Semtob	...	key hair stylist

Production Management

R.J. Louis	...	unit production manager
Harish Pujari	...	production manager

Second Unit Director or Assistant Director

Katie Carroll	...	dga trainee
David R. Ellis	...	second unit director (as David Ellis)
Michael Green	...	first assistant director: second unit
David Michael Katz	...	second assistant director: second unit (as David Katz)
Alicia Lewis	...	dga trainee
Dennis Maguire	...	first assistant director

Jayson Merrill ... key second assistant director
Andy Spilkoman ... second second assistant director

Art Department

Craig Abele ... model maker
Donna Ekins Kapner ... art department coordinator
Dana Yuricich ... sculptor: model maker
Gregory P. Alcus ... on-set dresser
Scott M. Anderson ... assistant property master
Kim Bailey ... technology design
Melanie J. Baker ... assistant art director
Richard Berger ... set designer
Richard K. Buoen ... concept illustrator
Robert Carbajal ... painter
Tony Chavez ... propmaker
Peter Clemens ... set designer
Mick Cukurs ... set designer
Jon Danniells ... lead man
Dale DeStefani ... foreman
Jeff Frost ... sculptor
Giacomo G. Ghiazza ... storyboard artist
Sam Greenmun ... prop construction
Keith Haynes ... Welder
Eric Hill ... set dresser
Chris Hopkins ... sculptor
Daniel R. Jennings ... set designer
Glen Kennedy ... set dresser
Mark Knapton ... foreman
Brian Massey ... set dresser
Ron Mendell ... set designer
James Miller ... lead sculptor (as Jamie Miller) / lead sculptor
David M. Milstien ... swing gang
David W. Mosher ... sculptor
Simon Murton ... conceptual artist
Edward V. Pannozzo ... set estimator
Ralph Peterson ... general foreman
Edmond Scott Ratliff ... set dresser
Clare Scarpulla ... set designer

Tom Shaw Jr.	...	property master
Mike Sudrow	...	weapons specialist
Bart Sullivan	...	set dresser
James Van Houten	...	sculptor
Freddy Waff	...	set dresser
Suzan Wexler	...	set designer
Joe Wood	...	construction coordinator
Deborah Wood	...	Labor Foreman
Feng Zhu	...	concept designer
Michael Denering	...	scenic artist (uncredited)
Sean Hood	...	set dresser (uncredited)
Kris Nagle	...	welder foreman (uncredited)
Wil Rees	...	production illustrator (uncredited)
Anthony Syracuse	...	foreman (uncredited)

Sound Department

Neal J. Anderson	...	dialogue editor (as Neal Anderson)
Bob Beher	...	foley editor (as Bob Behr)
Barbara J. Boguski	...	adr editor (as Barbara Boguski)
Bryan Bowen	...	sound effects editor (as Brian Bowen)
David E. Campbell	...	re-recording mixer (as David Campbell)
Paul Timothy Carden	...	supervising dialogue editor
Gail Clark Burch	...	adr editor
Donavan Dear	...	boom operator
Victor Ray Ennis	...	first assistant sound editor
Scott Martin Gershin	...	sound designer / sound effects editor
Mark Gordon	...	foley editor
Eric Gotthelf	...	foley mixer
Philip A. Hess	...	foley editor
Chris Hogan	...	foley editor (as Christopher Hogan)
Constance A. Kazmer	...	adr editor
Randy Kelley	...	sound effects editor
Tony Lamberti	...	sound effects editor
Lee W. Lebaigue	...	assistant sound editor
Peter J. Lehman	...	sound effects editor (as Peter Lehman)
Dave McMoyler	...	supervising adr editor
Glenn T. Morgan	...	sound effects editor (as Glenn Morgan)
Philip D. Morrill	...	assistant sound editor (as Phil Morrill)

Rick Morris	...	sound effects editor
Gary Mundheim	...	foley editor (as Gary Munheim)
Tony Negrete	...	assistant sound editor (as Tony R. Negrete)
Mark Ormandy	...	additional sound
Michelle Pazer	...	assistant sound editor
Michael A. Reagan	...	sound designer / sound effects editor
John T. Reitz	...	re-recording mixer (as John Reitz)
Gregg Rudloff	...	re-recording mixer
Mark P. Stoeckinger	...	supervising sound designer / supervising sound editor
Von Varga	...	cable person
Andy Wiskes	...	sound mixer
Peter Zinda	...	sound effects editor
Mark Johnston	...	sound recordist (uncredited)
Ken S. Polk	...	re-recording mixer (uncredited)

Special Effects by

John S. Baker	...	special effects
Marc Banich	...	special effects foreman
Michael Binczek	...	special effects
Al Broussard	...	special effects supervisor: second unit
Wayne Burnes	...	special effects technician
David Cohen	...	spray foam technician
Werner Hahnlein	...	special effects supervisor
William D. Harrison	...	special effects supervisor (as Bill Harrison)
Richard L. Hill	...	pyrotechnician
Donald Krause	...	special effects technician
Jerry Macaluso	...	additional animatronics: animatronic snake
Al Marangoni	...	pyrotechnician
Hans Metz	...	special effects supervisor
Clay Pinney	...	special effects supervisor
Joshua Pinney	...	special effects technician
Michael Roundy	...	special effects technician
Robert Simokovic	...	special effects supervisor
Keith Suzuki	...	special effects technician
Kenneth Van Order	...	special effects technician
Tom von Badinski	...	special effects technician
Tim Walkey	...	special effects foreman

Mike Wever	...	special effects technician
Ross Young	...	special effects
John Fleming	...	special effects technician (uncredited)
Alan Roberts	...	special effects technician (uncredited)
Robert Wilcox	...	crawler builder (uncredited)

Visual Effects by

Victor Abbene	...	chief lighting technician: visual effects
Erik Akutagawa	...	scan/record coordinator
David Altenau	...	technical director
Chris Anderson	...	visual effects coordinator (as Christopher Anderson)
Craig Barron	...	visual effects supervisor: Matte World Digital
Cory Bedwell	...	digital effects artist
Jon A. Bell	...	digital artist (as Jon Bell)
Justin Blaustein	...	projectionist: Rhythm & Hues
Casey Cannon	...	visual effects producer: BFTRE
Tom Capizzi	...	digital artist
Nadine Casamayou	...	assistant editor: BftRE
Mitzi Casida-Jones	...	visual effects producer
Dominick Cecere	...	CG animator
Jae Chang	...	technical director: Rhythm & Hues
Daniel Aristoteles Collins	...	systems/operations: Rhythm & Hues
Michael Conelly	...	sequence supervisor
Nick Danger	...	visual effects welder
Julian de la Pena	...	electrician: visual effects lighting
Krystyna Demkowicz	...	executive in charge of production: Matte World Digital
Diane Fazio	...	digital effects producer: Rhythm & Hues
Mark Felt	...	compositor
Adam Francis	...	motion control technician
Mark Franco	...	visual effects executive producer: Rainmaker Digital
Harrison Gibbs	...	visual effects editor
Brent Gilmartin	...	visual effects artist
Kelly Granite	...	visual effects compositor

Brian Hanable	...	digital effects compositor
John Hughes	...	studio head: Rhythm & Hues
Ian Hulbert	...	digital artist: Rhythm & Hues
Hitoshi Inoue	...	visual effects editor: BFTRE
Ed Jones	...	visual effects supervisor
Jongo	...	lighting technical director
John Joyce	...	lead model maker: Cinema Production Services
Michael Joyce	...	miniature supervisor: Cinema Production Services (as Mike Joyce)
B.L. Jurgens	...	visual effects technical director: Rhythm & Hues (as Bruce Jurgens)
Tex Kadonaga	...	modeler: Rhythm & Hues
Alisa Loren Klein	...	compositor
Tad Krzanowski	...	special model effects supervisor
Travis Langley	...	digital artist: BFTRE
Tom Leeser	...	visual effects supervisor: Rhythm & Hues
Patrick Lin	...	motion control camera operator: Matte World Digital
Van Ling	...	visual effects supervisor: BFTRE
Joe Mancewicz	...	animation setup
Ian Marks	...	digital artist: BFTRE
Will McCoy	...	digital compositor
Gregory Nic Nicholson	...	motion control operator
Timothy Niver	...	model maker
Brett Northcutt	...	digital matte artist
Hideki Okano	...	effects artist: Rhythm and Hues Studios
Chris Paxson	...	motion control technician
Jeryd Pojawa	...	lead modelmaker: Cinema Production Services, Inc.
Janet Quen	...	digital effects artist
Geoff Richardson	...	visual effects compositor: Matte World Digital
Paul Rivera	...	digital compositing supervisor: Matte World Digital
Mark Ross-Sullivan	...	lead modelmaker: Cinema Production Services, Inc.

Josh Saeta	...	digital artist: BFTRE
Marc-Andre Samson	...	digital artist
Gunther Schatz	...	digital 3-D artist: BFTRE
Tom Shaughnessy	...	miniature director of photography (as Tom J. Shaughnessy)
Kerry Shea	...	production manager: BFTRE
Christopher Sjoholm	...	digital supervisor: Rhythm & Hues (as Chris Sjoholm)
Kevin Andrew Smith	...	technical director
Martha Soehendra	...	digital artist: BFTRE
Suponwich Juck Somsaman	...	digital artist
Mark Spatny	...	visual effects production manager: POP Film
David Stump	...	miniature director of photography
Ken Swenson	...	lead modelmaker: Cinema Production Services, Inc.
David Taritero	...	visual effects producer: Pacific Title
Derick Tortorella	...	technical supervisor: BftRE
Morgan Trotter	...	3D artist
R. Gern Trowbridge	...	best boy electric: visual effects unit
Doug Tubach	...	digital effects supervisor: Rainmaker Digital Pictures
Todd Vaziri	...	compositing supervisor: BFTRE
Chris Waegner	...	digital effects artist
Jeff Wells	...	digital effects artist: Pacific Title/ Mirage
Terry Whiteside	...	visual effects producer: models and miniatures
Bob Wiatr	...	digital effects compositor
Gail Wise	...	production manager: BFTRE
Craig Andujar	...	prop maker (uncredited)
Olivier Barbeau	...	lighter (uncredited)
Todd Fellows	...	model maker: Cinema Production Services (uncredited)
Lynn Garrido	...	model maker: WKR (uncredited)
Jack M. Guberman	...	lamp operator (uncredited)
Alexandra Menapace	...	motion control operator (uncredited)
Aung Min	...	digital effects artist (uncredited)

Patrick Murphy	...	digital compositor: Rainmaker Digital Pictures (uncredited)
Brian Ringseis	...	cg artist (uncredited)
Michael Root	...	digital compositor (uncredited)
Amy Ryan Gunson	...	digital artist: Rhythm & Hues (uncredited)
Robert Small	...	visual effects (uncredited)
Kim Smith	...	model maker: miniatures unit (uncredited)

Stunts

Seth Arnett	...	stunts
Cheryl Bermeo	...	stunts
Chris Blackwood	...	stunts
May Boss	...	stunts
Janet Brady	...	stunts
Todd Bryant	...	stunts
Joe Bucaro III	...	stunts (as Joseph Bucaro III)
William H. Burton Jr.	...	stunts (as William H. Burton)
Chip Campbell	...	stunts
Keith Campbell	...	stunts
Jack Carpenter	...	stunts
John Casino	...	stunt double: Kurt Russell
Mark Chadwick	...	stunts
Jared Chandler	...	stunts
John T. Cypert	...	stunts (as John Cypert)
Mark De Alessandro	...	stunt coordinator: second unit / stunts
Chris Durand	...	stunts
Jared S. Eddo	...	stunts (as Jared Eddo)
Annie Ellis	...	stunts
Cindy Ellis	...	stunts
Tawny Ellis	...	stunts (as Tawny Marie Ellis)
Jeannie Epper	...	stunts (as Jeanie Epper)
Greg Fitzpatrick	...	stunts
Tim Gilbert	...	stunts
Troy Gilbert	...	stunts
James M. Halty	...	stunts (as Jim Halty)

Gary Harding Jr.	...	stunts
Riley Harper	...	stunts
Thomas Robinson Harper	...	stunts (as Tom Harper)
Greg Harris	...	stunts
Thirl Haston	...	stunts (as Thirl R. Haston)
Dana Hee	...	stunts
Steve Holladay	...	stunts
Buddy Joe Hooker	...	stunts
Norman Howell	...	stunts
Greg Isaacs	...	stunts
Steven Ito	...	stunts
Viktor Ivanov	...	stunts (as Victor Ivanov)
Kevin L. Jackson	...	stunts (as Kevin Lamont Jackson)
Cinda-Lin James	...	stunts (as Cindi-Lin James)
Shawn Kautz	...	stunts
Dennis Keiffer	...	stunts
Steve Kelso	...	stunts
Henry Kingi Jr.	...	stunt double: Jason Scott Lee
Svetla Krasteva	...	stunts
Khristian Lupo	...	stunts
Kent W. Luttrell	...	stunts (as Kent Luttrell)
Lisa McCullough	...	stunts
Dwayne McGee	...	stunts
Cliff McLaughlin	...	stunts
Dustin Meier	...	stunts (as Dustin J. Meier)
John Meier	...	stunts (as John C. Meier)
Rich Minga	...	stunts
Bennie Moore	...	stunts (as Bennie E. Moore)
Michael Munoz	...	stunt actor
Harry O'Connor	...	stunts
Jane Oshita	...	stunts
Steve Picerni	...	stunts
Don Pulford	...	stunts
Rex Reddick	...	stunts (as Rex J. Reddick)
Larry Rippenkroeger	...	stunts
Shawn Robinson	...	stunts
Troy Robinson	...	stunts
Danny Rogers	...	stunts

J.P. Romano	...	stunts
Jimmy Romano	...	stunts
Pat Romano	...	stunt rigger / stunts (as Patrick Romano)
R.A. Rondell	...	stunts
Debby Lynn Ross	...	stunts
John Rottger	...	stunts
James Ryan	...	stunts
Tom Schultz	...	stunts
Dane Selznick	...	stunts
Robin Tracey Sherwood	...	stunts (as Robin Sherwood)
Lincoln Simonds	...	stunts (as Lincoln P. Simonds)
Paul Sklar	...	stunts
John Maddox Smith	...	stunts
Sven-Ole Thorsen	...	stunts
Benny Urquidez	...	stunts
P.J. Wagner	...	stunts
April Weeden	...	stunts
Peter Weireter	...	stunts
Jeff Winn	...	stunts
Danny Wynands	...	stunts
Dick Ziker	...	stunt coordinator
Benny Urquidez	...	fight trainer (uncredited)

Camera and Electrical Department

Bobby Burton	...	chief lighting technician
Gary Capo	...	director of photography: second unit
Pat Dames	...	best boy grip: second unit
Damon Doherty	...	rigging grip
Allen D. Easton	...	camera operator: "a" camera
Bob Hall	...	first assistant camera: "a" camera
Paul Hazard	...	electrician
Erik Hecomovich	...	rigging grip
Robert Heine	...	assistant camera
Casey Jones	...	key grip
Eric K. Jones	...	second assistant camera
James Keys	...	rigging gaffer

Jason Kilgore ... rigger
Brian Lataille ... remote head operator: stab-c
Allen Marshall ... electrician
Wayne Marshall ... best boy electric
Peter McAdams ... grip
Mark Mele ... rigging gaffer
Parker Meyer ... film loader: second unit
Brad Peterman ... first assistant camera: "a" camera, second unit
Ron Phillips ... still photographer
Glen Purdy ... best boy rgging grip
David Schmalz ... video assist operator
Philip Shanahan ... second assistant camera
Ty Suehiro ... key rigging grip
Jesse Tango ... best boy electric: second unit
Mark Van Loon ... camera operator
Lance Jay Velazco ... video assist operator
Donald J. Vos ... best boy grip
Charles W. Wayt ... dolly grip
Dale White ... second assistant camera: "b" camera
Joel White ... grip
Steven J. Winslow ... assistant camera: Wescam camera / camera technician
Barry Berona ... assistant camera (uncredited)
Eli Golub ... assistant camera (uncredited)
Michael Maloney ... rigging grip (uncredited)

Casting Department

Julia Kim ... casting associate

Costume and Wardrobe Department

Francesca Bruno ... costumer
Christopher Gilman ... wardrobe: specialty costumes
Donna Marcione Pollack ... costume supervisor
Joseph T. Mastrolia ... set costumer (as Joe Mastrolia)
Katrina Mastrolia ... set costumer
Muto-Little ... costume maker
Mark Peterson ... costume supervisor

John M. 'Jack' Wright ... set costumer
Clark Acton ... Model Maker: Space Suits (uncredited)
William Iversen ... model maker: space suits (uncredited)

Editorial Department

Elaine C. Andrianos ... first assistant editor
Stacey S. Clipp ... second assistant editor
Lorinda Donovan ... second assistant editor
Mo Henry ... negative cutter
David Orr ... color timer
Bill Daly ... post-production executive (uncredited)
Brandon K. Hogan ... post-production (uncredited)
Margaret Liu ... assistant editor (uncredited)

Location Management

Mike Fantasia ... location manager
Michael Wesley ... assistant location manager (as Michael Wesley Aycock)

Music Department

Tom Boyd ... musician: oboe soloist
Tom Brown ... music preparation
Wade Culbreath ... musician: percussion
Alex Gibson ... music editor
Daniel Gold ... music prep
Jim Hoffman ... Music Preparation
Brian Kilgore ... musician: percussion
Norman Ludwin ... musician: bass
Joel McNeely ... conductor
Shawn Murphy ... music score mixer / music score recordist
Maria Newman ... musician
Denise Okimoto ... assistant music editor
John Rodd ... orchestral scoring recordist
Curtis Roush ... music editor
Dennis Sager ... scoring engineer
Marni Sanders ... copyist
David Slonaker ... orchestrator

Steven L. Smith ... music preparation
Ron Aston ... musician: percussion programming (uncredited)
John Beal ... composer: trailer (uncredited)

Script and Continuity Department

Heather Harris ... script supervisor: second unit
Lyn Matsuda Norton ... script supervisor (as Lyn Norton)

Transportation Department

Linda Cipperley ... transportation
Vic Cuccia ... transportation captain
Randy Luna ... driver
David Oppenheim ... driver: production van
Jim Petti ... driver: cast
Dan Romero ... transportation coordinator
Randy White ... transportation captain
Dean Winton ... driver
Alberto Coto ... driver (uncredited)
Mitch Friedman ... driver (uncredited)

Additional Crew

Kimberly Aguirre ... payroll accountant
Scott M. Anderson ... asst. prop master
Toni Atterbury ... unit publicist
Ruth Auerbach ... studio teacher
Jared Chandler ... armorer
David Cohen ... mold maker foreman
Karine Cruz ... production associate
Paul Emmons ... rigging medic
David Fencl ... armorer
Carol Gans ... studio teacher
Sam Greenmun ... combat suit technician
Fran Joseph ... fight choreographer: Mr. Lee
Kim Pinkstaff ... assistant: Jerry Weintraub
Jerry Poteet ... fight choreographer: Mr. Lee
Jeffrey D. Stevens ... first aid / key set medic
Ken Twohy ... key set production assistant

Julie Wagner	...	stand-in: Connie Nielsen
Jeff Winn	...	craft service
Michael Crawford	...	post-production accountant (uncredited)
Eli Golub	...	technician: HotHead (uncredited)
Matthew Howard	...	adr loop group (uncredited)
John Tomko	...	production executive (uncredited)

Index

Made in the USA
Middletown, DE
26 May 2023

31038291R00086